WHEN JUSTICE
IS ABORTED

D1519223

Other books by Gary North

Marx's Religion of Revolution, 1968 [1988]
An Introduction to Christian Economics, 1973
Unconditional Surrender, 1981
Successful Investing in an Age of Envy, 1981
The Dominion Covenant: Genesis, 1982
Government By Emergency, 1983
The Last Train Out, 1983
Backward, Christian Soldiers?, 1984
75 Bible Questions Your Instructors Pray You Won't Ask, 1984
Coined Freedom: Gold in the Age of the Bureaucrats, 1984
Moses and Pharaoh: Dominion Religion Versus Power Religion, 1985
Negatrends, 1985
The Sinai Strategy, 1986
Conspiracy: A Biblical View, 1986
Unholy Spirits: Occultism and New Age Humanism, 1986
Honest Money, 1986
Fighting Chance, 1986 [with Arthur Robinson]
Dominion and Common Grace, 1987
Inherit the Earth, 1987
The Pirate Economy, 1987
Liberating Planet Earth, 1987
Healer of the Nations, 1987
Is the World Running Down?, 1988
Puritan Economic Experiments, 1988
Political Polytheism: The Myth of Pluralism, 1989
Tools of Dominion: The Case Laws of Exodus, 1989
Pollution: A Biblical View, 1989
Slavery: A Biblical View, 1989
Victim Rights: A Biblical View, 1989
Trespassing for Dear Life, 1989

Books edited by Gary North

Foundations of Christian Scholarship, 1976
Tactics of Christian Resistance, 1983
The Theology of Christian Resistance, 1983
Editor, *Journal of Christian Reconstruction* (1974-1981)

WHEN JUSTICE IS ABORTED

Biblical Standards for Non-Violent Resistance

Gary North

Dominion Press
Fort Worth, Texas

When Justice Is Aborted: Biblical Standards for Non-Violent Resistance

Copyright © 1989 by Gary North

Appendix B reprinted with permission from **Grand Illusions: The Legacy of Planned Parenthood**, by George Grant. (Wolgemuth and Hyatt, Publishers, Inc., Nashville, Tennessee.)

Typesetting by Nhung Pham Nguyen

Printed in the United States of America

ISBN 1-55926-124-2

This book is dedicated to

Joan Andrews

who was the victim of injustice
because she was not accompanied by
a sufficient number of dedicated,
risk-taking peers.

TABLE OF CONTENTS

Our Nation cannot continue down the path of abortion, so radically at odds with our history, our heritage, and our concepts of justice. This sacred legacy, and the well-being and the future of our country, demand that protection of the innocents must be guaranteed and that the personhood of the unborn be declared and defended throughout our land. In legislation introduced at my request in the First Session of the 100th Congress, I have asked the Legislative branch to declare the "humanity of the unborn child and the compelling interest of the several states to protect the life of each person before birth." This duty to declare on so fundamental a matter falls to the Executive as well. By this Proclamation I hereby do so.

NOW, THEREFORE, I, RONALD REAGAN, President of the United States of America, by virtue of the authority vested in me by the Constitution and laws of the United States, do hereby proclaim and declare the unalienable personhood of every American, from the moment of conception until natural death, and I do proclaim, ordain, and declare that I will take care that the Constitution and laws of the United States are faithfully executed for the protection of America's unborn children. Upon this act, sincerely believed to be an act of justice, warranted by the Constitution, I invoke the considerate judgment of mankind and the gracious favor of Almighty God. I also proclaim Sunday, January 17, 1988, as National Sanctity of Human Life Day. I call upon the citizens of this blessed land to gather on that day in their homes and places of worship to give thanks for the gift of life they enjoy and to reaffirm their commitment to the dignity of every human being and the sanctity of every human life.

IN WITNESS WHEREOF, I have hereunto set my hand this fourteenth day of January, in the year of our Lord nineteen hundred and eighty-eight, and of the Independence of the United States of America the two hundred and twelfth.

Ronald Reagan

PREFACE

Be strong and of a good courage: for unto this people shalt thou divide for an inheritance the land, which I sware unto their fathers to give them. Only be thou strong and very courageous, that thou mayest observe to do according to all the law, which Moses my servant commanded thee: turn not from it to the right hand or to the left, that thou mayest prosper whithersoever thou goest. This book of the law shall not depart out of thy mouth; but thou shalt meditate therein day and night, that thou mayest observe to do according to all that is written therein: for then thou shalt make thy way prosperous, and then thou shalt have good success. Have not I commanded thee? Be strong and of a good courage; be not afraid, neither be thou dismayed: for the LORD thy God is with thee whithersoever thou goest (Joshua 1:6-9).

This passage is a familiar one. God was sending the second generation of liberated Israelites into a seven-year military conflict, the war for the Promised Land. The first generation had died in the wilderness, except for Joshua and Caleb, and now Joshua was about to lead Israel into battle. The first generation had refused to fight, and had been ready to stone Joshua and Caleb for saying that God would give them the victory (Numbers 14). God had killed them for their lack of faith, as He had promised almost forty years earlier.

Say unto them, As truly as I live, saith the LORD, as ye have spoken in mine ears, so will I do to you: Your carcases shall fall in this wilderness; and all that were numbered of you, according to your whole number, from twenty years old and upward, which have

ix

murmured against me. Doubtless ye shall not come into the land, concerning which I sware to make you dwell therein, save Caleb the son of Jephunneh, and Joshua the son of Nun. But your little ones, which ye said should be a prey, them will I bring in, and they shall know the land which ye have despised. But as for you, your carcases, they shall fall in this wilderness (Numbers 14:28-32).

God had imposed His national negative sanctions against them for their personal and corporate cowardice and lack of faith in Him. Now Joshua was the new national leader. His claim almost forty years earlier was about to be vindicated by God.

Notice the five major points of God's instruction to Joshua. First, God, the sovereign Lord of history, is commanding them. He is present with them. Second, He refers to Moses, His representative and national leader over Israel, in His instructions to Joshua, His new representative and national leader. Third, He tells Joshua to honor and obey the law of God. Fourth, He tells him that if he and the people obey this law, they will prosper. Fifth, He tells him that they will inherit the land.

This is the Bible's five-point covenant model. God reminded Joshua of all five points before He led them into battle. It was on the basis of this covenant and its promises that Joshua was expected to have courage.

When Christians face a corporate challenge to their faith, they must exercise corporate responsibility. Today, Christians are in a war, a war against secular humanism. The leaders of the humanist camp are far more self-conscious about this war than most Christians are. This is why they have an initial advantage. But that advantage can and will be overcome as Christians rediscover their heritage of successful resistance to tyranny. The recovery of this heritage must begin with an understanding of the biblical covenant model.

Faithful Christians should no longer ignore the comprehensive nature of this war. The enemy's army is advancing toward us whether we acknowledge it or not. It has been advancing since the day that Satan entered the garden. Let us not be so foolish or naive as Eve was when the first shots of this ethical and judicial war were fired.

But let us also not forget that this enemy army is now governed by a new strategy, a strategy of counter-attack. Jesus Christ at Calvary inflicted a mortal head wound on the enemy commander, as predicted by God (Genesis 3:15). Satan's forces are now fighting a defensive battle, like Germany at the Battle of the Bulge in late 1944. This battle looks like an offensive campaign, but it is really defensive. When Christians at last realize the full implications of the resurrection and ascension of Christ to heaven, and the sending of the Holy Spirit to His people, they will launch a series of offensive campaigns in every battlefield of life. They will "mop up" the enemy.

Until Christians do begin to take the resurrection seriously, they will find themselves on the defensive. But these defensive battles can be won. Let me give you an example.

The Nebraska School War, 1981-84

In 1982, Pastor Everett Sileven of the Faith Baptist Church of Louisville, Nebraska was thrown in jail. What was his crime? Refusing to hire state-licensed teachers and use a state-authorized curriculum in his church's school. As headmaster, he had refused to comply with state regulations for several years. In 1982, the Sheriff of Cass County walked into a Sunday School class one Sunday morning and served him with a subpoena. The war had gone to stage two.

Fortunately, the church had purchased a videotape camera and recorded this and a whole series of outrages that were to follow. These media-compelling segments received national attention through television, although primarily on secular television reports. The "Eyewitness News" crowd cannot resist "hot" videotapes of live action, since eyewitness news is so seldom actually eyewitness news. As it turned out, this videotape camera was crucial to the church's remarkable victory in Nebraska. Anyone who fails to recognize the power of this simple tool in a media war probably does not understand that public confrontations are inescapably media wars. Not only is such a naive person unlikely to win the media war, he is probably not going to get involved in one. "Too unspiritual," you understand.

Not all the Christian media "got on board" the Louisville school case, sad to say, although the 700 Club did produce a couple of reports on the crisis. The popular "we're high on Jesus" T.V. shows refused, as usual, to take sides. Too controversial. It might hurt the ratings. (Five years later, national controversy hit two of these national television ministries and damaged all the rest. At least two Christian media representatives would have been wiser to have spent more time covering the Nebraska school war and less time uncovering their consorts.)

Cass County ordered the church's school closed. When Rev. Sileven refused, the county threw him in jail. As word of his arrest spread, accompanied by an emotionally moving videotape of the sheriff hauling him off to jail, hundreds of pastors around the country began to stream into tiny Louisville. They were not famous pastors. Famous pastors stayed discreetly silent. They were pastors of small congregations who recognized how vulnerable their churches and schools were.

Local residents deeply resented these "outside agitators" in the same way that white residents in the South hated the freedom riders and protesters in the early 1960's. The local residents of Louisville, Nebraska, like local residents everywhere, worship their public schools, whether or not they worship God or attend church. They tithe their children to the state in these schools, generation after generation; very few of them tithe to a church. Rev. Sileven was calling into question the morality and legality of the entire system of state licensing of private schools, and he was gaining national attention for this protest against this universally accepted tyranny. The State of Nebraska was being made to look foolish in the eyes of the nation, and it was Sileven who was the cause of this. So, Rev. Sileven and his supporters became *persona non grata* in Louisville, Nebraska.

Meanwhile, the respectable churches of Nebraska stayed safely quiet. If they had a Christian school — and few did — their schools were safely registered with the state and had been for years. Sileven was making a moral and legal issue out of a law that they had capitulated to years earlier. Sileven would get no support from these churches.

The state legislators were outraged that anyone would challenge the state laws that made it almost impossible to start a Christian high school, and that greatly restricted the operation of small day schools. What business was it of these outsiders? What business was it of the national evening news teams? They resented all these "outside agitators." Most of all, they resented the media attention their tyranny was receiving.

This war was fought and won on television and in the courts. That much became clear by late 1984. It was becoming clearer in 1983.

The local county judge grew frightened and stepped down from the case. The county brought in another judge from a nearby county to continue the pressure. His name, astoundingly, was Ronald Reagan. He cracked down on the school. The battle was escalating around the state. Twenty other schools also refused to comply. Pastors were being sent to jail. Half a dozen fathers in Sileven's church were sent to jail. Sileven was released from jail, but then was threatened with imprisonment again for contempt of court. He fled across the state line into Iowa in the fall of 1983. His adult daughter, a teacher in the school, also had to flee the state. This was war.

The visiting pastors began holding nightly prayer meetings. Under court authorization, the sheriff and his men ordered these pastors to leave the church one night. The pastors refused. The sheriff then sent his men into the church and dragged out dozens of pastors. This was stupid. Really stupid. It was all being videotaped. The reaction of the sheriff to the action of the pastors created a classic media event. This videotaped reaction led to the next phase of the war.

The sheriff was media perfect. It was as if he had been sent in from central casting. A big, gruff, arrogant man, he looked every inch a bully. It was clear on camera that he was not about to pay any attention to the civil rights of Christians. All he cared about was that he had been authorized by Cass County to shut down this little church school, and if necessary, the church itself, and if this meant dragging a bunch of praying pastors out of the church, well so much for the power of prayer.

Rev. Ed Rowe had written a paperback book about the events of 1982: *The Day They Padlocked the Church* (Huntington House, 1983). The wonders of modern printing technology were put to use in a righteous cause. So were the technological wonders of videotape. The edited videotape of the police dragging pastors out of the church was used to mobilize other churches around the nation. The church was immediately re-opened. The war escalated. Hundreds of pastors streamed into Louisville.

Visiting pastors now began to pray Psalm 83 against the sheriff and the county government. Christians are not familiar with Psalm 83. They need to be. It includes this section:

> Do unto them as unto the Midianites; as to Sisera, as to Jabin, at the brook of Kison: Which perished at En-dor: they became as dung for the earth. Make their nobles like Oreb, and like Zeeb: yea, all their princes as Zebah, and as Zalmunna: Who said, Let us take to ourselves the houses of God in possession. O my God, make them like a wheel; as the stubble before the wind. As the fire burneth a wood, and as the flame setteth the mountains on fire; So persecute them with thy tempest, and make them afraid with thy storm. Fill their faces with shame; that they may seek thy name, O LORD. Let them be confounded and troubled for ever; yea, let them be put to shame, and perish: That men may know that thou, whose name alone is JEHOVAH, art the most high over all the earth (Psalm 83:9-18).

The pastors prayed other similar psalms (called "imprecatory psalms) and prayers. They took turns as teachers in the school. They took turns as "co-headmasters" of the school. Some of them even brought their children from out of state to enroll, just to give the kids an opportunity to take part in an historic event.

In response to the preliminary phases of this Nebraska school war, I decided in 1982 as co-editor of *Christianity and Civilization*, a scholarly journal being published by Geneva Ministries of Tyler, Texas, to produce a journal dealing with Christian resistance. I sent out letters to prospective authors, asking them if they had anything to contribute. I was flooded with responses. Eventually, we published two volumes: *The Theology of Christian Resistance*, which was over 350 pages, and *Tactics of Christian Resistance*, which was almost 500 pages. I carried copies of the second volume to Nebraska when I visited in early December of 1983. I wrote up the story in the December 16, 1983 issue of my newsletter *Remnant Review*.

I immediately received cancellations from "Christian conservatives" in Nebraska. They were outraged at my report. I was uninformed, they said. Sileven was a troublemaker and an outlaw, they said. We should all leave Nebraska alone, they said.

For weeks, revolving teams of twenty pastors each had gone to the governor's office for a meeting. "I will not meet with those lawbreakers," he vowed. These groups still came to his office, week after week. At last, he met with them. Then, in desperation over the national media coverage and also about the state's inability to shut down the schools, he created a blue ribbon commission of experts from outside the state to study the matter. Much to the legislature's consternation, the panel said the state was way, way out of line. That was the beginning of the end for the State of Nebraska's war on Christian schools.

Next, a lawyer provided to the church by a national Christian ministry sued in Federal District Court and won. The county had indeed violated the First Amendment rights of the pastors when the sheriff dragged them out of that prayer meeting. Next, the sheriff had a heart attack and resigned.

Finally, the state capitulated. It passed a law that virtually freed Christian schools from all state control. The "outside agitators" had won. Through their efforts as His representatives, God, the ultimate Outside Agitator, had also won.

But all the way to the finish line, the vast majority of the churches in Nebraska (and everywhere else) had remained silent. They had not wanted trouble. They had preferred to capitulate silently to evil. They were like the cowardly tribes of Israel of whom Deborah sang: "Gilead abode beyond Jordan: and why did Dan remain in ships? Asher continued on the sea shore, and abode in his breaches" (Judges 5:17). It was only the little people and little churches that protested. The respectable folks in Nebraska stayed at home in the fall of 1983 to watch Nebraska's number-one rated college football team on television. The season was capped by a trip to the January 1, 1984 Orange Bowl, where Nebraska lost by one point in the final minute, shattering the dreams and vicarious egos of "Cornhusker" fans for another year. God is not mocked.

At least two pastors whom I met at the meeting in Nebraska told me that their state boards of education were watching the Nebraska protest very closely. The pastors said that if the Christians lost in Nebraska, their states were ready to crack down on unregistered Christian schools. But the state lost in Nebraska, and Christian schools around the nation received several years of breathing room.

Christians had protested. They had run a successful challenge to a well-entrenched humanist tyranny. Nebraska's Board of Education had been tyrannical throughout the century. It was Nebraska which, in a "patriotic" fury during World War I, restricted the teaching of foreign languages in the public schools, since the most popular foreign language was German. With very little support from the Christian community, locally or nationally, and with many arrests and the dedicated opposition of both the state and local civil government, Christians won the battle in 1984.

This precedent should not be forgotten today.

Operation Rescue

Beginning in the summer of 1988, we began to see a replay of those 1983 protests. This time the issue was abortion. The war has now escalated dramatically. Operation Rescue has begun to mobilize Christians around the United States. Christians are standing in the doorways of profit-seeking abortion mills in order to keep murderous mothers from their accomplices, the state-licensed, state-protected, U.S. Supreme Court-authorized abortionists. They intervene in the name of God and the unborn victims. They *interpose* their bodies between the mothers and the physicians.

Once again, the local communities that have passively allowed these murderous abortion mills to flourish are complaining about "outside agitators." Once again, the Christian community is divided. Once again, fearful, conventional, and respectable churches have refused to bless these tactics of non-violent resistance, fearing local controversy more than they fear the wrath of God over murdered babies. Once again, the media has proven crucial to the conflict.

And once again, the question has been raised by the critics, especially the Christian critics: "By what authority are these people breaking the law?" *When Justice Is Aborted* is an answer to this question, whenever and wherever it is raised.

I wrote this book in six working days. I had sent out a flyer by Randall Terry, the organizer of Operation Rescue, in the October 1988 mailing of my Institute for Christian Economics (P.O. Box 8000, Tyler, TX 75711). I received a letter from a pastor regarding this flyer. Why had I sent this? Didn't I know about Operation Rescue's tactics? This pastor has long been publicly opposed to abortion. If he was ready to call Operation Rescue's tactics into question, it was time to provide some explicitly biblical answers.

Of course, I already had. The two volumes of *Christianity and Civilization* were five years old in 1988. But the first was out of print, and the few copies remaining of the second, on tactics of

Christian resistance, were forgotten. Something else was needed, something shorter, cheaper, and easier to read.

I started the manuscript of this book on October 29, a Saturday morning, took Sunday off, and finished the first draft on the following Wednesday. I sent photocopies by overnight mail to several Christian leaders. Two leaders then suggested that I write an appendix refuting published criticisms of Operation Rescue, which I did the following week. That took an extra day. I spent another day tinkering with the manuscript to prepare a final draft. So, this book was basically a one-week operation. That I could do this in one week is a testimony to the power of the biblical covenant model, the Word Perfect 4.2 word processing program, and the Godspeed computerized Bible search program.

Once you understand the Bible's five-point covenant model, you can solve lots of intellectual, moral, and judicial problems fairly easily. In fact, once you memorize this model, you will recognize it again and again as you read the Bible. Much of the Bible is structured in terms of this model. Once it gets into your mind, it does not get out. Without this model, biblical solutions are far more difficult to come by. So, I strongly suggest that you take this five-point model seriously, keeping it in mind as you read your Bible, and turning to it whenever you are called upon to defend what you are doing in the name of Jesus Christ.

INTRODUCTION

Let me offer you a series of scenarios. All of them are drawn from church history. Christians in the real world had to make decisions in the light of their faith. What decisions would you have made? What decisions *should* you have made?

The year is 150 A.D. You live in the city of Rome. Roman civil law says that the father is the supreme ruler in his family. He has the legal right to abandon unwanted infants that are born in his household. The common practice is for these infants to be abandoned outside the gates of the city. It has become the practice of Christians to pick up these abandoned babies and take them home to rear as their own children. The Roman civil authorities have declared this practice illegal. You are walking home and find one of these babies. Should you obey the civil law and ignore the child? Or should you break the law by taking it home?

The year is 298. Emperor Diocletian's persecution of the church is in full force. The civil authorities are rounding up all copies of the Bible from Christian churches. You are the pastor of a local church. The authorities learn of this and come to your home, demanding that you turn over any copy of the New Testament which you in fact do possess. You have copies of several epistles and two of the gospels hidden in your home. They ask you if you own such books. Should you tell them the truth?

Christians for centuries disobeyed these laws. In the year 313, Emperor Constantine issued the Edict of Milan, declaring religious toleration for Christianity.

The year is 1941. You are a Christian living in German-occupied Holland. You have been approached by a Jewish family seeking refuge from the Nazis. It is illegal to hide Jews, but they ask you to hide them. Should you tell them to look for refuge elsewhere, since you do not want to break the law?

The year is 1944. The Nazis have been informed that all Christians are required by God to tell the truth no matter what the circumstances. They have believed this story. So, they are going from door to door, asking every known church member if he knows where any Jews are being hid by others. You, a faithful Christian, know that your non-Christian neighbor is illegally hiding a Jew in the attic. German soldiers come to your door and ask you point blank: "Do you know if anyone in this neighborhood is hiding Jews?" If you answer no, the soldiers will probably leave, knowing that you are unlikely to lie. If you tell them yes, you will be asked where the Jews are. If you say nothing, they will know you know. They will arrest you for withholding evidence, and they will also conduct a detailed search of the neighborhood. Should you lie, tell them the truth, or remain silent?

Christians in Holland disobeyed the Nazis throughout World War II. On April 30, 1945, Adolph Hitler committed suicide in Berlin.

It is Thursday, December 1, 1955. You live in the city of Montgomery, Alabama. You are a black woman coming home from a hard day's work. You are sitting on a bus in the front section, which is legal as long as no white person is required by crowding to sit next to you. By city law and local bus line rules, blacks are not allowed to sit parallel to a white. The bus fills up. A white man is standing at the front of the bus because there are no more seats available. The bus driver tells you to get up and move to the back of the bus; a white person needs the seat. You are required to get up and let him sit there. You will have to stand at the back of the bus. But you have paid your fare, and your local taxes support the municipal bus line. Should you stand up and move to the back of the bus?

It is Saturday, December 4. You are a black person living in Montgomery. You learn that a lady named Rosa Parks was arrested the day before yesterday for refusing to give up her seat and stand in the back of the bus. You hear that blacks are organizing a boycott of the local bus company until the seating rule is abolished. They are saying, "If we can't sit wherever we want to, on a first-come, first-seat basis, we won't spend our money to ride the bus. We should be treated just like any other passengers." The boycott will begin on Monday morning. Should you join the boycott and refuse to ride the bus?

It is Monday, December 12. The leaders of the boycott are mainly ministers. The boycott is working. The buses are 75% empty. But the local authorities have discovered an obscure state law that makes it illegal to run a boycott against any state or municipal service. You are a black person who owns an automobile. Many blacks have joined the boycott and are seeking alternative ways to get to work in the morning and back home at the end of the day. You are asked by a representative of the boycotting group to drive people to work and back home in the evening. The city has said this is illegal, since there is a city ordinance requiring a minimum fee for all "taxi" service, and you will be regarded as a taxi service. Should you agree to drive people anyway?

Rosa Parks and the blacks of Montgomery defied the law. On December 17, 1956, the U.S. Supreme Court refused to hear a protest by the City of Montgomery against a Federal appellate court's ruling that the segregated seating was illegal. Bus segregation ended in Montgomery on December 21, 1956, a little over a year after Mrs. Parks sat tight and broke the law.

The year is this year. You know that a local abortion clinic is killing unborn babies. You know that the civil government has authorized such murder if it is performed by a monopolistic, state-licensed physician. Picketing has been tried; it has not stopped the murdering from going on. Christians have decided that if a large number of them block the doorway to the clinic, it will make it more difficult for mothers to murder their infants. It will lead to financial losses for the clinic. It also could become a tremendous media event in which the absolute brutality of abortion is reflected in the brutality of the local police against protesters. But to block the doorway is an invasion of the clinic's private property. The protests have begun, and the police have started arresting those who block the doorway. Should you approve of the protest or not? If you approve, should you join the protest or not? If you suspect that the police will escalate their physical violence against protestors, should you join the protest? If you get arrested, should you later insist on a jury trial or meekly forfeit the bail you posted in order to be released?

If no Christians protest, will the abortion laws ever be changed?

What If a Civil Law Is Biblically Immoral?

The civil government could declare a particular act illegal which in God's eyes is legal or moral. The civil government could also declare something legal which in God's eyes is illegal or immoral. How can those under the authority of the specific civil government in question persuade the civil authorities to bring the law into harmony with God's law?

The first step is for Christians to accept the fact that *there really is such a thing as God's law*. If Christians deny this, then their protests are in vain. They must first seek explicitly biblical answers to the question: "By what judicial and moral standard?"

Second, Christians must decide which doctrines and practices are most important in God's hierarchy of values and requirements. The color of the drapes is less important than the purity of doctrine. Most Christians say that they believe this. But what about *applied doctrine*? What about a question like abortion? What if a church preaches sound doctrine but attempts to stay neutral about abortion? There is no neutrality in God's world, of course, but there is lots of attempted neutrality. (There surely also is a great deal of indifference.) Christians must decide which unjust laws to obey and which to disobey, since no one can fight every aspect of civil injustice at one time. We are creatures. No one has sufficient time or resources to fight every possible battle. There must be a division of labor and specialized protests by various Christian groups.

The third step in deciding what must be done to persuade the civil magistrates is a *question of tactics*: either cease obeying the law as a means of establishing a judicial test case or else seek to change the law by political means, and obey a bad law as a matter of public relations until all legal political efforts to abolish it have failed. Both approaches have been used in history. The former approach is by far the most common, obviously so in non-democratic societies, but even in democratic societies. The English Revolution of 1688 and the American Revolution of 1776 were both fought to establish the right of the people to escape bad rulers and bad laws.

Someone usually must disobey a law if it is to be changed. The legitimacy of laws is established or rejected in the courts. If the law has been issued in the name of the sovereignty of the people, then the best way to persuade the legal spokesmen of the people that they have misrepresented the people is for the people to disobey the law.

Someone has to begin this process of disobedience. When he does, it will not be clear to everyone that "the people" are about to "speak." Only time will tell.

If God says that a law is wrong, then Christians know that eventually – if only at the day of judgment – the law will be changed. But God usually persuades civil magistrates of the immoral nature of their laws long before the day of final judgment. He first destroys their power in history, sometimes by destroying their nation. The Old Testament is filled with examples of this. A Christian who publicly disobeys a law that is condemned by the Bible is taking a major step in delaying the wrath of God on his society. Disobedience to bad laws is therefore an act of patriotism. But it will be criticized as an act of anarchism.

How can Christians distinguish between legislation-defying acts of anarchism and legislation-defying acts of patriotism? Only by going to the Bible to test the spirits of disobedience. Above all, we must understand that *the Bible is a covenantal document.* To understand the difference between good and evil, we must understand what God's covenant is.

The Covenant Structure

To get the right answers, we need first to ask the right questions. For a long, long time, Christians and Jews have had the correct questions right under their noses, but no one paid any attention. The questions concerning lawful government are organized in the Bible around a single theme: *the covenant.*

Most Christians and Jews have heard the word "covenant." They regard themselves (and occasionally even each other) as covenant people. They are taught from their youth about God's covenant with Israel, and how this covenant extends (or doesn't extend) to the Christian Church. But not many people who use the word really understand it. If you go to a Christian or a Jew and ask him to outline the basic features of the biblical covenant, he will not be able to do it rapidly or perhaps even believably. Ask two Jews or two Christians who talk about the covenant, and compare the answers. The answers will not fit very well.

In late 1985, Pastor Ray Sutton made an astounding discovery. He was thinking about biblical symbols, and he raised the question of two New Testament covenant symbols, baptism and communion. This raised the question of the Old Testament's covenant symbols, circumcision and passover. What did they have in common? Obviously, the covenant. But what, precisely, is the covenant? Is it the same in both Testaments (Covenants)?

He began rereading some books by theologian Meredith G. Kline. In several books, Kline mentioned the structure of the Book of Deuteronomy. He argued that the book's structure in fact parallels the ancient pagan world's special documents that are known today as the suzerain treaties. These treaties were imposed by conquering kings on defeated kings who were offered the opportunity to become vassals of the conqueror.

That triggered something in Sutton's mind. Kline discusses the outline of these treaties in several places. In some places, he says they have five sections; in other places, he indicates that they may have had six or even seven. It was all somewhat vague. So Sutton sat down with Deuteronomy to see what the structure is. He found five parts.

Then he looked at another book of the Bible that is known to be divided into five parts: Matthew. He believes that he has found the same structure. Then he went to other books, including some Pauline epistles. He found it there, too. When he discussed his findings in a Wednesday evening Bible study, author David Chilton instantly recognized the same structure in the Book of Revelation. He had been working on this manuscript for well over a year, and he had it divided into four parts. Immediately he went back to his computer and shifted around the manuscript's sections electronically. The results of his restructuring can be read in his marvelous commentary on the Book of Revelation, *The Days of Vengeance* (Ft. Worth, Texas: Dominion Press, 1987).

Here, then, is the five-point structure of the biblical covenant, as developed by Sutton in his path-breaking book, *That You May Prosper: Dominion by Covenant* (Tyler, Texas: Institute for Christian Economics, 1987).

1. The transcendence yet presence of God
2. Hierarchy/representation (government)
3. Ethics/law (dominion)
4. Oath/sanctions (blessings and cursings)
5. Succession/inheritance (continuity)

Simple, isn't it? Its acronym is THEOS. Simple though it is, it has many important implications. *Here is the God-revealed key that unlocks the structure of every human government.* Here is the biblically mandated model of government that Christians can use to analyze church, state, family, and numerous other non-covenantal but contractual institutions.

The first five books of the Bible, the Pentateuch, conform to this five-point outline. Genesis tells us who God is: the sovereign creator who is transcendent, yet fully present with His people. Exodus tells about God's hierarchical government (especially in Exodus 18), with Moses as God's representative. Leviticus sets forth the laws of the sacrifices. Numbers tells the story of God's sanctions against the disobedience of Israel and also against the pagan nations that Israel battled against. Finally, Deuteronomy is the second reading of God's law, just before the second generation entered the land of Canaan to possess the inheritance promised to Abraham. I discuss all this in greater detail in the Introduction to my commentary on Genesis, *The Dominion Covenant: Genesis*, second edition (Institute for Christian Economics, 1987).

This five-point model can be used to unlock the long-debated structure of the Ten Commandments: 1-5, with a parallel 6-10. I spotted this almost as soon as Sutton described his discovery, just as I was finishing my economic commentary on the Ten Commandments, *The Sinai Strategy: Economics and the Ten Commandments* (Institute for Christian Economics, 1986). I outlined this covenantal structure of the Ten Commandments in the Preface. James Jordan has demonstrated that the Book of Leviticus also follows this five-point structure in his book, *Covenant Sequence in Leviticus and Deuteronomy* (Institute for Christian Economics, 1989).

You may not be confident that the Bible really teaches such a view of the covenant. One way to test the thesis is to examine the rival covenants that are described in the Bible. If they are also structured in the same way, then we have additional evidence that this structure is universal.

Covenant vs. Covenant

The Book of Exodus is the premier book of the covenant (Ex. 24:7). It therefore bears the marks of all five aspects of the biblical covenant model. The first chapter of Exodus indicates that a war between rival covenants was the heart of the dispute between God and Pharaoh. Pharaoh attempted to impose his own alternative covenant on the Hebrews. It, too, had the same five aspects, and his confrontation reveals all five. This covenant structure appears twice in the first chapter: a double witness.

The first presentation of the Pharaoh's covenant program appears in the Bible's description of his general rule over the Hebrews. First, transcendence/presence: the book begins with the advent of a false god, the Pharaoh who had forgotten Joseph (Ex. 1:8). Second, hierarchy: this false god immediately established a tyrannical hierarchy over the people of Israel, with "taskmasters to afflict them with their burdens" (v. 11). Third, law: he forced them to build treasure cities for him (v. 11). But their afflictions led to even greater growth in their population (v. 12), threatening Pharaoh's program of dominion. Fourth, sanctions: he announced a program of infanticide (v. 16). Fifth, inheritance: he was seeking to destroy their inheritance in the land by killing their male children, but allowing the females to survive — an attempt to capture the inheritance of Israel through future concubinage. Egypt would marry Israel, God's bride, steal the bride's God-granted dowry, and declare her a concubine.

The second presentation of the Pharaoh's covenant program appears in the Bible's description of his enforcement of the infanticide decree. To achieve this program of stealing the Hebrews' inheritance, Pharaoh (the self-proclaimed sovereign) assigned this task of infanticide to representative agents, the Hebrew midwives (hierarchy). He gave them a command: destroy the newborn males (law). They disobeyed the command, but instead of being punished by Pharaoh (negative sanction), God blessed them (positive sanction). And the Hebrew people multiplied (inheritance).

In response to the false Egyptian covenant, the sovereign God of Israel announced to Moses that He was with His people, for He had seen their afflictions and had heard their cries (Ex. 3:7). He then raised up Moses, his representative agent, to serve as the earthly leader of the nation (hierarchy). He gave Moses His laws (law). The people made an oath to God, which they broke, and God brought sanctions against them (oath/sanctions). They then repented, renewed the covenant, and built the tabernacle, which their sons later carried into the Promised Land, the lawful inheritance which had been promised to Abraham (inheritance/ continuity).

Thus, we see that the confrontation between Moses and Pharaoh was really a confrontation between rival covenants. They both had the same five-point model. The same confrontation between God's covenant and Satan's rival covenant is going on today.

Rival Covenants Today

We live in an era of humanism. Humanism is a simple enough religion. The humanist believes the following:

1. Man owns the earth. Original ownership, meaning the original title to the earth, belongs to collective mankind. It is "his" to use as "he" pleases.
2. Man the creature rules God the Creator. In fact, man *is* the creator, for he alone understands and controls nature through science. He runs the show.
3. Man, therefore, makes the rules, which means that an elite group of men make the rules for everyone else. "Man proposes, and man disposes." He alone is to subdue the earth.
4. Man is the sovereign judge of the universe. He answers only to man, which means of course that the vast majority of men answer to a handful of other men, the elite: scientific, political, and bureaucratic.
5. The future belongs to autonomous (self-ruled) man, meaning to those people who worship man as God. Autonomous man inherits the earth.

Christians disagree with each of the above humanist assertions.

1. Original ownership belongs to God. God, not man, created, owns, and controls the earth.
2. The Creator rules the creature. God is sovereign. God has delegated subordinate ownership to mankind. God is in charge.
3. God, therefore, has made the rules (laws). Men prosper or fail in terms of their obedience or disobedience to these rules.
4. God judges man in terms of His law. Men are responsible before

God to abide by His rules. Man proposes and disposes only within the decree and plan of God.

5. The future belongs to God and God's people. Those who are meek before God will inherit the earth.

Here we have it: two rival religions, two rival views of God, with the earth as the historical battlefield. The religion of God and the religion of man are locked in deadly combat. But the humanists have had a much clearer view of the true nature of the battle. They have planned for it far longer than the Christians have.

The Covenant Lawsuit

The prophets of the Old Testament were authorized agents of God. They were His prosecuting attorneys. They brought a covenant lawsuit against the nation. They reminded the people, the nobles, and the king of the covenant that God had made with their forefathers at Sinai. Then they reminded the listeners of the stipulations (laws) of that original covenant. They pointed to the obvious violations of these stipulations in their day. Then they warned everyone of the fact that God, the true king of Israel, would bring His negative sanctions against the nation: war, pestilence and famine. All of these negative sanctions had been spelled out in the original covenant document (Deuteronomy 28:15-68). Finally, the prophets called the nation to repentance, promising the blessings of God — positive sanctions (Deuteronomy 28:1-14) — if the nation did repent. Understand, these sanctions — positive and negative, blessings and cursings — were applied corporately to the whole nation. They were not simply sanctions against personal sins. When the two parts of the nation were sent into captivity, righteous people as well as evil people were taken out of the land.

This office of prophet culminated in the person of Jesus Christ. His cousin John had brought a preliminary covenant lawsuit against Israel. He then baptized Jesus. From that point on, Jesus brought the main covenant lawsuit against Israel. (John was executed when he brought God's personal covenant lawsuit against Herod and his wife.) When Israel refused to repent, God raised up His church. Not only was the church required to bring covenant lawsuit against Israel, it was required to bring the same lawsuit against the whole world. This was why Paul was raised up to go to the Gentiles (Acts 13), and why Peter was sent to the Roman centurion (Acts 10).

What this means is that *the covenant that God made with Israel has now been extended by God to the whole world.* God today calls all men to repentance. All people are now clearly under the ethical terms of the covenant (God's Bible-revealed laws). Thus, it is the task of Christians to warn people of the nature of this covenant — a sovereign God, a hierarchical system of governments, biblical laws, God's sanctions in history and eternity, and God's system of inheritance and disinheritance. In short, Christians are to preach the gospel.

But we are not just to preach it verbally. We are to preach it by our deeds. God requires *word-and-deed evangelism.* One of these visible deeds is our resistance to publicly sanctioned evil. This is as true today as it was during the Old Testament.

Stages of Biblical Resistance

The Bible reveals numerous cases of lawful, righteous protests against civil authority. They are not all of the same intensity. I present here a series of steps that seem to me to be progressive, depending on time and place. It may be that under different circumstances, several of them might be interchangeable. But this guide at least serves as an introduction to the question of the stages of lawful resistance.

First, there is the case of an individual who knows that a law is wrong, and who protests verbally. He obeys it, but he warns the civil magistrate that it is an immoral law and recommends that it be repealed. Joab did this when David insisted that the people be numbered in a military census, even though there was no battle scheduled (II Samuel 24:3-4). For this sin, God sent a plague on Israel that killed 70,000 people (II Samuel 24:25). (This story affirms the biblical doctrine of representative hierarchical government. The king sinned, and the people suffered the terrible consequences: physical sanctions. But Joab, who had protested, was spared.)

Second, the protester protests verbally and refuses to obey the order. The protester then voluntarily suffers the punishment. This is what the three young men did when Nebuchadnezzar told them to worship the image or suffer death in the fiery furnace (Daniel 3).

Third, the protester rebels against civil authority, warning the civil ruler of the evil that he is doing, but then leaves the geographical jurisdiction of the civil government. This is what Elijah did when he warned the king about God's coming judgment of drought, and then hid in the city of Zarephath in the nation of Sidon (I Kings 17).

Fourth, the protester refuses to comply with the law. He recognizes that there is no institutional way to protest, and because of his unique position in being able to deflect the evil consequences of the law, he or she adopts the strategy of deception rather than personal emigration. The best examples in the Bible of this approach are the deception of Pharaoh by the Hebrew midwives (Exodus 1) and the deception of Jericho's authorities by Rahab (Joshua 2).

Fifth, the people as a corporate assembly intervene and tell the ruler (executive) that he will not be allowed to bring sanctions in order to enforce a bad law. The people of Israel did this when they refused to allow Saul to execute Jonathan for having eaten some honey during a battle, which Saul had previously prohibited (I Samuel 14:43-46).

Sixth, a God-anointed protester warns the representatives of the people and challenges them to rebel against lawfully constituted authority. This is what Elijah did when he directed the assembled representatives of Israel to kill the 850 priests of Baal and Asherah after God had publicly intervened in history to prove that these priests were false priests (I Kings 18:40).

Seventh, the God-ordained lower official joins with other officials and revolts against unlawful central government after a series of official protests. This is what Jeroboam did when Rehoboam, Solomon's son, imposed harsh new taxes (or possibly a system of forced labor). Jeroboam created a new nation, the northern kingdom of Israel. "So Israel rebelled against the house of David unto this day" (I Kings 12:19).

We should also consider the question of lawful resistance against a military invader. Ehud the judge slew King Eglon of Moab through the use of deception (Judges 3:15-26). He then called the nation to a military revolt (Judges 3:27-30). Similarly, Jael deceived the fleeing Canaanitic general Sisera, even though her husband (a higher covenantal authority) had made some sort of peace treaty with Sisera (Judges 4:17). She rammed a peg through his temple until it nailed him to the ground (Judges 4:21) – a graphic symbolic fulfillment of God's promise to crush the head of the serpent (Genesis 3:15). For this act of successful military aggression and household covenantal rebellion, Deborah praised Jael in her song of victory (Judges 5:24-27).

There is no indication in the Bible that any of these acts was morally or judicially improper, and in most cases, God granted visible positive sanctions as rewards for such action. Anyone who says that resistance and even revolution (rebellion) are not morally and judicially justified in the Bible has to ignore or deny a great deal of Scripture, and also renounce the legitimacy of the English Revolution of 1688 and American Revolution of 1776, as well as renounce the various anti-Nazi national underground resistance efforts during World War II.

Reader, are you ready to do this?

Conclusion

The many questions surrounding the big question of lawful resistance by Christians against immoral civil laws can be answered by a careful examination of the biblical covenant model. I have divided this book into five chapters, with each chapter structured in terms of one of the five points. I hope Christians will better understand what they are being called to do in this age of seemingly triumphant secular humanism. If Christians cannot see the life-and-death issue of abortion, then they are not prepared to exercise dominion in any area of civil government.

R. J. Rushdoony wrote a little pamphlet called *Abortion is Murder* in 1971, two years before the U.S. Supreme Court handed down the infamous *Roe v. Wade* decision. Few Christians noticed the pamphlet. Two years later, in 1973, Rushdoony's *Institutes of Biblical Law* was published. This book identified the historical background of modern abortion. Abortion is a revival of a moral issue that brought Christians into conflict with ancient pagan Rome. There was no reconciliation possible between Rome and the Church, between the pagan Caesar and Christ. It was only settled when Christians took over the Roman Empire.

> In Biblical law, all life is under God and His law. Under Roman law, the parent was the source and lord of life. The father could abort the child, or kill it after birth. The power to abort, and the power to kill, go hand in hand, whether in parental or in state hands. When one is claimed, the other is soon claimed also. To restore abortion as a legal right is to restore judicial or parental murder (p. 186).

Christians must now make up their minds: Are they going to assent to legalized murder or oppose it publicly? Are they going to break the civil law as a means of challenging it as a test case, or are they going to allow humanists to continue to authorize the murder of babies? The U.S. Supreme Court has overturned its own prior rulings at least 150 times. Are Christians ready to give the Court an opportunity to do it again?

Note to the Reader

I have filled this book with quotations from the Bible. This is necessary, since so many Christian critics of social action and especially direct confrontation insist — legitimately, I might add — that those who propose non-violent protests present an explicitly biblical case for what they are doing. While I draw upon examples from history, I use them only as examples. I am making a biblical case for civil disobedience, not a "natural law" case or a historical case. The Bible is my sole authoritative standard.

This means that those Christians who want to understand my arguments are going to be required to read carefully my sometimes lengthy extracts from the Bible. If they are unwilling to do this, they are prepared to be neither critics nor advocates of my position. We must count the cost of what we are doing. Understanding the biblical basis of our actions is part of the cost.

1

THE AUTHOR OF ALL AUTHORITY

And he changeth the times and the seasons: he removeth kings, and setteth up kings: he giveth wisdom unto the wise, and knowledge to them that know understanding (Daniel 2:21).

When a Christian asks himself the question, "Why should I obey an immoral law?", he has taken the first step in developing a theory of Christian social ethics.

When he asks himself the question, "How far should I go in obeying an immoral law?", he has taken the first step on the road to social activism.

When he asks himself the question, "In what way should I oppose an immoral law?", he has taken the first step on the road to Christian resistance.

A Christian wants to please God. He does not want to do evil. Is obeying an evil civil law itself evil? He cannot answer this question accurately unless he has a concept of social ethics. Usually this concept is merely implicit; Bible-believing Protestants have not thought very much about developing an explicitly Bible-based social ethics since the early 1700's. The initial question is where the Christian should begin his search for social ethics: "Why should I obey an immoral law?" He needs a biblically valid way to discover an accurate, God-honoring answer to this question.

It is really the question of sin and its control over men and institutions. Christians are in the world, but we are not of the world (John 17:10-19). By "of the world," Jesus meant our place

17

of *origin*. We are spiritual creatures. Our spiritual origin is outside this world. Christians are citizens of heaven (Philippians 3:20). Yet we are also citizens of this world. We are subject to a higher heavenly power and also to lower earthly powers. We make ethical decisions in this world, and these decisions have implications for at least our starting position in the next world (I Corinthians 3).

The questions begin. How did these earthly powers gain lawful authority over us? By what legal right do they exercise authority over us if they command us to obey evil laws, or refuse to prosecute evil acts, thereby delivering us into the hands of evil people? Thus, the second step in developing a Christian applied ethical system is to get a biblical answer to the question: "What is the source of all earthly authority?"

We should begin our search with the most fundamental pair of questions a person can ask: "Who is God, and what does he want me to do?"

God the Sovereign Creator

God is absolutely sovereign. He is the Creator. "I have made the earth, and created man upon it: I, even my hands, have stretched out the heavens, and all their host have I commanded" (Isaiah 45:12). He sustains the universe providentially through His Son, Jesus Christ. It is God the Father who "hath delivered us from the power of darkness, and hath translated us into the kingdom of his dear Son: In whom we have redemption through his blood, even the forgiveness of sins: Who is the image of the invisible God, the firstborn of every creature. For by him were all things created, that are in heaven, and that are in earth, visible and invisible, whether they be thrones, or dominions, or principalities, or powers: all things were created by him, and for him: And he is before all things, and by him all things consist" (Colossians 1:13-17).

God answers to no one except Himself. No one holds God accountable for what He has done or has failed to do. "Wilt thou also disannul my judgment? Wilt thou condemn me, that thou mayest be righteous?" (Job 40:8). He is the author of all human authority, the ultimate voice of authority. What He says goes. He speaks, and it comes to pass. "Thus shall mine anger be accomplished, and I will cause my fury to rest upon them, and I will be comforted: and they shall know that I the LORD have spoken it in my zeal, when I have accomplished my fury in them. . . . So it shall be a reproach and a taunt, an instruction and an astonishment unto the nations that are round about thee, when I shall execute judgments in thee in anger and in fury and in furious rebukes. I the LORD have spoken it. . . . So will I send upon you famine and evil beasts, and they shall bereave thee; and pestilence and blood shall pass through thee; and I will bring the sword upon thee. I the LORD have spoken it" (Ezekiel 5:13, 15, 17). When God speaks, the world had better listen.

We do not live in a world of random events. All things happen in terms of God's plan for the ages. The universe is *personal*, not impersonal. It reflects God. "For the invisible things of him from the creation of the world are clearly seen, being understood by the things that are made, even his eternal power and Godhead; so that they are without excuse" (Romans 1:20).

No Other God

God's claims regarding Himself are all-inclusive. He is the only God. "I am the LORD, and there is none else, there is no God beside me: I girded thee, though thou hast not known me: That they may know from the rising of the sun, and from the west, that there is none beside me. I am the LORD, and there is none else" (Isaiah 45:5-6).

The kings and rulers of this world despise this view of God. They are at war with God, and they ridicule anyone who preaches that such a God exists. They insist that there is no transcendent God. If there were such a God, then they would not be totally sovereign. Their word would not be the standard of authority in history. So, they rebel against Him by publicly denying that He exists. They join in a conspiracy against the God they say is not here and cannot be. "Why do the heathen rage, and the people imagine a vain thing? The kings of the earth set themselves, and the rulers take counsel together, against the LORD, and against his anointed, saying, Let us break their bands asunder, and cast away their cords from us" (Psalm 2:1-3). God in turn laughs derisively at them. "He that sitteth in the heavens shall laugh: the Lord shall have them in derision. Then shall he speak unto them in his wrath, and vex them in his sore displeasure" (Psalm 2:4-5).

Because God's claims are all-inclusive, all rival claims of absolute sovereignty are false. Yet the rulers of this world make such claims. *There is a political-theological war going on throughout history.* This war is between two groups of people: covenant-keepers and covenant breakers. There is no way to reconcile these two groups. Each side tries to persuade the other side to join the "true" cause, but neither side believes that there can ever be more than a truce or temporary cease-fire between them in history. *This is a war for the hearts and minds of men. It is also inevitably a war for the lawful control over all of mankind's institutions.* There is not one grain of sand, not one soul, not one seat of authority, that is outside this battlefield.

What is the official god of any society? *A society's god is its publicly designated source of law.* Thus, a society's legal order will testify to the nature and character of its god. The legal order will support that god and its followers. The law will say "yes" to those activities that the society's god says "yes" to; it will say "no" to everything that the god says "no" to. *There can be no civil law without a public "yes" and "no."* Civil law inevitably promotes one group's goals for society and suppresses other groups' goals. This is why there can be no religious neutrality in history. This is also why there can be no religious neutrality in politics and civil law.

There can be only one voice of absolute authority in society. There is only one source of legitimate law. There is one God, and only one, who will succeed in bringing His comprehensive will to pass in history. This is the God of the Bible. Those who claim to be His followers are required to acknowledge His absolute sovereignty. But they cannot do this without simultaneously denying all other gods, all rival claims to absolute sovereignty. They may be forced to obey laws that another god has declared, but they must always deny the claims of divinity — final sovereignty — of all such gods.

No Higher Loyalty

The early Christians were law-abiding citizens. Their leaders claimed that they were the most law-abiding citizens in the land. But this did not impress the Caesars. The Christians were obstinate. They refused to worship the other gods in the Roman pantheon. They refused to offer incense to the "genius of the Emperor" at public altars. As the claims to divinity by the emperors increased as the decades rolled on, so did their hostility to the Christians. While persecutions were intermittent, the emperors always maintained their official hostility to the Christians. Christians were seen as a subversive force in Rome, not because they were *violent* revolutionaries, which they were not, but because they were *inward* revolutionaries. They were outward revolutionaries, too, for they refused to take an active part in the rites of the Emperor cult. Religious resistance was understood in the ancient classical world as political revolution, for classical religion was political, and politics was inescapably religious.

It was the religiously exclusive nature of Christianity that drew the authorities' hatred. Rome's religion grew more and more inclusive. The gods of the various conquered nations all had a place in the Roman pantheon. None, however, was allowed to claim absolute sovereignty. Absolute sovereignty was the sole possession of the Emperor, as the highest political figure in the empire. Rome's religion, like the city states of Greece, was ultimately a political religion. It was not the gods of Olympus that men actively worshipped; it was the local household god, the tribal god, and the god of the city-state. Eventually, it was the god of Rome, the Emperor.

Jesus' Denial of All Rival Loyalties

Jesus Christ denounced all loyalties that challenged His ultimate authority. He denounced family loyalties first and foremost,
for the family was the most important rival covenantal unit, the
one loyalty to which men throughout most of history have been
most likely to place at the head of their list of loyalties.

> Behold, I send you forth as sheep in the midst of wolves: be ye
> therefore wise as serpents, and harmless as doves. But beware of
> men: for they will deliver you up to the councils, and they will
> scourge you in their synagogues; And ye shall be brought before
> governors and kings for my sake, for a testimony against them and
> the Gentiles. But when they deliver you up, take no thought how
> or what ye shall speak: for it shall be given you in that same hour
> what ye shall speak. For it is not ye that speak, but the Spirit of
> your Father which speaketh in you. And the brother shall deliver
> up the brother to death, and the father the child: and the children
> shall rise up against their parents, and cause them to be put to
> death. And ye shall be hated of all men for my name's sake: but
> he that endureth to the end shall be saved (Matthew 10:16-22).

> Whosoever therefore shall confess me before men, him will I
> confess also before my Father which is in heaven. But whosoever
> shall deny me before men, him will I also deny before my Father
> which is in heaven. Think not that I am come to send peace on
> earth: I came not to send peace, but a sword. For I am come to set
> a man at variance against his father, and the daughter against her
> mother, and the daughter in law against her mother in law. And
> a man's foes shall be they of his own household. He that loveth
> father or mother more than me is not worthy of me: and he that
> loveth son or daughter more than me is not worthy of me (Matthew
> 10:32-37).

Christians prefer social and institutional peace to open warfare. At the same time, they recognize that the clash of religious
principles is inevitable. They insist on elevating the name of God
above all other names. "Be it known unto you all, and to all the
people of Israel, that by the name of Jesus Christ of Nazareth,
whom ye crucified, whom God raised from the dead, even by him

doth this man stand here before you whole. This is the stone which was set at nought of you builders, which is become the head of the corner. Neither is there salvation in any other: for there is none other name under heaven given among men, whereby we must be saved" (Acts 4:10-12). This is deeply resented by the apostles of other loyalties, other gods.

Comprehensive Salvation and Social Action

Without this elevating of the name of Jesus Christ, there can be no personal salvation, nor can there be social salvation, meaning social *healing*. (A salve is a healing ointment; the English word "salvation" is related to the English word for healing.) God heals all men in history; therefore He saves them. "For therefore we both labour and suffer reproach, because we trust in the living God, who is the Saviour of all men, specially of those that believe" (I Timothy 4:10). Not all men will go to heaven, but all men receive undeserved, unmerited, *life-healing blessings in history* through the grace of God in Christ. (We call this form of grace "common grace.")

This is why Christians who understand *the comprehensive nature of sin* must also preach *the comprehensive nature of salvation* in Jesus Christ. Because Adam's sin has tainted every aspect of life, the redemption which is offered by Jesus Christ, the last Adam (I Corinthians 15:45), in principle promises to cleanse every aspect of life. *The bodily resurrection of Christ in history testifies to the possibility of comprehensive restoration in history.* While sin is never perfectly conquered in history until the final judgment, Christians can work in confidence that their God is the God of history as well as eternity, and therefore their efforts in history, meaning *this side of Christ's Second Coming*, are not in vain in history.

The Promise of Restoration in History

The Book of Isaiah is full of promises regarding the future of God's people when they at last succeed in persuading men to covenant with God. Notice the language of righteousness and justice; this is the promise of salvation:

> And I will turn my hand upon thee, and purely purge away
> thy dross, and take away all thy tin: And I will restore thy judges
> as at the first, and thy counsellors as at the beginning: afterward
> thou shalt be called, The city of righteousness, the faithful city.
> Zion shall be redeemed with judgment, and her converts with
> righteousness (Isaiah 1:25-27).

> And many people shall go and say, Come ye, and let us go up
> to the mountain of the LORD, to the house of the God of Jacob; and
> he will teach us of his ways, and we will walk in his paths: for out
> of Zion shall go forth the law, and the word of the LORD from
> Jerusalem. And he shall judge among the nations, and shall rebuke
> many people: and they shall beat their swords into plowshares, and
> their spears into pruninghooks: nation shall not lift up sword
> against nation, neither shall they learn war any more. O house of
> Jacob, come ye, and let us walk in the light of the LORD (Isaiah
> 2:3-5).

> And the work of righteousness shall be peace; and the effect of
> righteousness quietness and assurance for ever. And my people
> shall dwell in a peaceable habitation, and in sure dwellings, and
> in quiet resting places (Isaiah 32:17-18).

> For brass I will bring gold, and for iron I will bring silver, and
> for wood brass, and for stones iron: I will also make thy officers
> peace, and thine exactors righteousness. Violence shall no more
> be heard in thy land, wasting nor destruction within thy borders;
> but thou shalt call thy walls Salvation, and thy gates Praise. . . .
> (Isaiah 60:17-18).

> Thy people also shall be all righteous: they shall inherit the
> land for ever, the branch of my planting, the work of my hands,
> that I may be glorified. A little one shall become a thousand, and
> a small one a strong nation: I the LORD will hasten it in his time.
> The spirit of the Lord GOD is upon me; because the LORD hath
> anointed me to preach good tidings unto the meek; he hath sent
> me to bind up the brokenhearted, to proclaim liberty to the cap-
> tives, and the opening of the prison to them that are bound; To
> proclaim the acceptable year of the LORD, and the day of vengeance

of our God; to comfort all that mourn; To appoint unto them that mourn in Zion, to give unto them beauty for ashes, the oil of joy for mourning, the garment of praise for the spirit of heaviness; that they might be called trees of righteousness, the planting of the LORD, that he might be glorified. And they shall build the old wastes, they shall raise up the former desolations, and they shall repair the waste cities, the desolations of many generations (Isaiah 60:21-61:4).

Jesus and the Jubilee Year

These prophetic passages in Isaiah 61 and 62 are tied to the benefits of the jubilee year, Israel's year of release (Leviticus 25). It was these verses that Jesus cited when He read from Isaiah in the synagogue at Nazareth.

> And he came to Nazareth, where he had been brought up: and, as his custom was, he went into the synagogue on the sabbath day, and stood up for to read. And there was delivered unto him the book of the prophet Esaias. And when he had opened the book, he found the place where it was written, The Spirit of the Lord is upon me, because he hath anointed me to preach the gospel to the poor; he hath sent me to heal the brokenhearted, to preach deliverance to the captives, and recovering of sight to the blind, to set at liberty them that are bruised, To preach the acceptable year of the Lord. And he closed the book, and he gave it again to the minister, and sat down. And the eyes of all them that were in the synagogue were fastened on him. And he began to say unto them, This day is this scripture fulfilled in your ears (Luke 4:16-21).

If the jubilee year was fulfilled by Christ in principle at the very beginning of His ministry on earth, then Christians should work hard to manifest this liberty principle in history. *The promised year of release is judicially behind us.* As free men in Christ, we should therefore strive to extend this covenantal kingdom freedom to all the nations of the earth. This is what preaching the gospel is all about: the comprehensive healing (salvation) of individuals and institutions.

To say that salvation is strictly limited to the hearts of men is to say that the manifestation of the glory of God in history is limited to the hearts of men. But this is not how the Bible speaks of salvation: "For Zion's sake will I not hold my peace, and for Jerusalem's sake I will not rest, until the righteousness thereof go forth as brightness, and the salvation thereof as a lamp that burneth. And the Gentiles shall see thy righteousness, and all kings thy glory: and thou shalt be called by a new name, which the mouth of the LORD shall name. Thou shalt also be a crown of glory in the hand of the LORD, and a royal diadem in the hand of thy God" (Isaiah 62:1-3).

God is seen through His people's actions and the institutions that they build to His glory in terms of His covenant. The presence of God is manifested by the visible working out of His kingdom's principles in history. It is a mistake to assume that God is not present just because He is not physically present. Such a view of the presence of God belittles the work of the Holy Spirit in history.

God Is Present With His People

Jesus promised after His resurrection: "Lo, I am with thee always, even unto the end of the world" (Matthew 28:20). He then ascended into heaven (Acts 1:9). But before He departed, He promised the disciples that "ye shall receive power, after the Holy Ghost is come upon you: and ye shall be witnesses unto me both in Jerusalem, and in all Judea, and in Samaria, and unto the uttermost part of the earth" (Acts 1:8).

This is one of the strangest facts in the Bible: in order for God to be present with His people in power, His Son had to depart from the earth. *Because Jesus Christ has departed physically, His people can be closer to God spiritually than if He had remained on earth.* Jesus was very clear in His teaching about this:

> But now I go my way to him that sent me; and none of you asketh me, Whither goest thou? But because I have said these things unto you, sorrow hath filled your heart. Nevertheless I tell you the truth; It is expedient for you that I go away: for if I go not away, the Comforter will not come unto you; but if I depart, I will

send him unto you. And when he is come, he will reprove the world of sin, and of righteousness, and of judgment: Of sin, because they believe not on me; Of righteousness, because I go to my Father, and ye see me no more; Of judgment, because the prince of this world is judged. I have yet many things to say unto you, but ye cannot bear them now. Howbeit when he, the Spirit of truth, is come, he will guide you into all truth: for he shall not speak of himself; but whatsoever he shall hear, that shall he speak: and he will shew you things to come. He shall glorify me: for he shall receive of mine, and shall shew it unto you. All things that the Father hath are mine: therefore said I, that he shall take of mine, and shall shew it unto you. A little while, and ye shall not see me: and again, a little while, and ye shall see me, because I go to the Father (John 16:5-16).

There are millions of Christians today who feel impotent in the face of this world's powers. They believe that because Jesus Christ is not physically present on earth that His people are at best people without much influence. Worse, they believe that as time goes on, God's people will have even less influence. They will be steadily surrounded and forced into the shadows of history.

Did Jesus say such a thing? No, He said that the prince of this world is judged. He said that He had to go away so that His people could gain more knowledge and more authority. He said that the Holy Spirit would lead godly men into all truth. But today's Christians cannot seem to understand the extent of the authority that Christ passed to His people when He sent the Holy Spirit into the midst of the church. Christians lack confidence because they do not fully understand the extent to which God is present with His people in their battles against the spiritual heirs of Satan. They believe that the only way for them to be salt and light and the leaven of righteousness in history is for Jesus to come again physically and set up an international Christian bureaucracy.

If this is not berating the work of the Holy Spirit, what is? If this is not ignoring the specific words of Jesus — that His people will receive power when the Holy Spirit comes to them — then what is? Today Christ's bodily resurrection is behind us. We have a completed Bible to teach us and the Holy Spirit to illuminate our minds. We have centuries of experience behind us through the development of church creeds and courts. We have nineteen centuries of missions experience to draw upon. We also possess vast economic wealth — capital undreamed of as recently as two centuries ago, or even half a century ago. We have incomparable tools of communication. What more do we lack? *Confidence!*

In spite of all these God-given tools of dominion, Christians feel as if they were a tiny besieged army surrounded by powerful hostile forces. When they read that the gates of hell shall not prevail against the church (Matthew 16:18) — the church prevails, not the angelic host of heaven — they somehow hear in their minds something quite different: that the gates of heaven will prevail against Satan's demonic onslaught. They think of Satan as being on the offensive today. They forget what the resurrection of Christ did to Satan. *They do not acknowledge that the resurrection of Jesus and the sending of the Holy Spirit changed anything fundamentally in history.* It is not clear in their minds that ever since Christ's resurrection and ascension to heaven, the church has been on the offensive, and Satan has been on the defensive.

Legitimate Confidence

With God above us and church history behind us, why should we Christians have doubts about the earthly success of our cause? We may have doubts regarding our own courage and capacities, but we should have none regarding God's strength. Psalm 110:1 makes God's plan plain: "The LORD said unto my Lord, Sit thou at my right hand, until I make thine enemies thy footstool." The fact that Jesus is seated at the right hand of God in heaven is not a guarantee of the church's progressive defeat until He returns again physically in absolute power; on the contrary, He sits at God's right hand *until* His enemies are subdued. The verse could not be any plainer. Jesus will not return again until the church, as His authorized representative in this New Testament era, has made His enemies His footstool. "Then cometh the end, when he shall have delivered up the kingdom to God, even the Father; when he shall have put down all rule and all authority and power" (I Corinthians 15:24).

We should believe that God wants to see His name elevated in history. The creation reflects Him; therefore, as history progresses, it should reflect God as the author of all human authority. How can His position as Lord over creation be manifested in history? Through the effective labor of His covenant people, even though Jesus is physically absent. He is surely not *judicially* absent! Dare we say that God the Father can manifest His position as sovereign Lord in history only by sending Jesus physically to dwell in some temple or government building? This sounds foolish on the face of it, yet millions of Christians today believe in something very close to this scenario.

Jesus Christ manifests His position as the Lord of history through His people. We are His representatives on earth, His ambassadors. To the extent that we extend our influence in His name, God's supreme authority is manifested in history. As we shall see in Chapter 2, God's authority in history is manifested *representatively*. Just as Jesus represented God in history, and just as the Holy Spirit represents both God the Father and Jesus Christ the Son, so does the community of "called-out" Christians represent God the Trinity. The church as an institution is Christ's body (Romans 12; I Corinthians 12). It represents God on earth.

Unless Christians view New Testament history in this light, they will be sorely tempted in two different ways: either to retreat from the confrontations in history or to become fanatics seeking martyrdom in a nesessarily suicidal confrontation with evil. Neither approach is justified by what the Bible teaches about the church's role in history. What Christians should conclude is that by prayer, covenantal faithfulness, patient hard work, courage to march forward, and evangelism by word and deed, the kingdom of Jesus Christ will be steadily extended in history. Christians are not called upon to become spiritual kamikazes, flying bomb-laden planes into the enemy's massive fleet of ships. On the contrary, we are supposed to be the massive fleet of ships into which Satan's fanatic suicide squadrons fly their planes. Satan is the supreme kamikaze pilot, not Jesus. Satan's followers are the fanatics on a suicide mission, not God's followers.

Because Christians today do not really believe in an absolutely transcendent sovereign God, they do not have the self-confidence that is required to build a kingdom. Because they do not believe that God is with them always, in every battle against evil, they do not want to get involved in any battle against evil that is outside the narrow confines of the local church or the family. But evil is out there, moving toward us, surrounding us. Unless we are ready and able to go on the offensive and take the war to the enemy wherever he is, the enemy will work to weaken us and then try to eliminate us from every seat of influence. It is time for Christians to go visibly on the offensive against public social evils.

The Gospel Is Confrontational

Christianity is in a war to the death with humanism — not just behind the Iron Curtain, but everywhere. There are a lot of Christians who hate the thought of this fight. They deny that it can be won by Christians. They are correct to this extent: it can't be won by those who hold to pietism's theology of the church's impotence in history. Such a theology weakens Christians' will to resist because it weakens their will to attack. But we have to fight to win. If a person will not fight to win, then he might as well surrender now and save himself a lot of trouble.

A lot of pietists today trust in the coming Rapture as the only way to escape the necessity of publicly surrendering to Satan and his earthly representatives. This means that in order to avoid the public embarrassment of an official surrender to Satan, God's people must leave civilization behind them historically and below them geographically. This is the eschatology of "up, up, and away!"

The Rapture is a legitimate hope regarding the end of time, but not in the middle of history. The problem is, millions of

Christians have already abandoned civilization psychologically and motivationally. They have trained themselves to think and act anti-culturally. Because they think of the Rapture as leading them to a safe and historically irresponsible ghetto in the sky, they have adopted a ghetto mentality today. They have packed their bags emotionally. They have learned to think as losers. They forget that God does not call us to surrender this civilization to His enemies. Western civilization is at stake. Those on the defensive in this battle for world civilization will lose. The best defense is a good offense. A good Christian offense must rely on biblical law and faith in Christianity's God-ordained victory in history.

Too many churches want peace. They want quiet. They don't want controversy. They never want to hear harsh words against their lethargy. Better to preach against unidentified sin, they think. Better to close one's eyes to the obvious. Better to die in one's sins. So, when we activist Christians disturb their self-imposed slumber, they call us harsh. Well, we should not care what they call us. History is forcing their hand. So is God.

A Comprehensive Gospel

Preaching a comprehensive gospel means confronting a fallen world with a vision and program for comprehensive redemption. This initially reduces the appeal of a simple "save me!" gospel, for it asks that people implicitly ask God: "Save me for your purposes!" By seeking to avoid the inhibiting effect that a realization of vast new responsibilities will have on the listeners — inhibiting apart from the Holy Spirit — preachers have offered a watered-down version of the gospel. It is a gospel without comprehensive covenantal responsibilities. What they ignore is that God's Spirit saves men wholly by the power of God. He does not save proportionately more people because the gospel message has been watered down. He saves just as many as He had chosen, "before the foundation of the world" (Eph.1:4).

Jesus said that we are to pray like a woman who seeks justice from an unjust judge (Luke 18:1-5). She comes to him again and again, until he finally settles the dispute. Now, is her incessant pestering of the judge useless? She is told to keep pestering him. For a long time, this produces nothing except sore knuckles from banging on the door. But those knuckles toughen up, and she learns patience. She learns to keep coming back. Eventually, the judge capitulates. He can stand it no longer. She, in turn, has received her gift — the discontinuous transformation of her circumstances — as a result of her continuous efforts.

The parable of the unjust judge and the persistent seeker of justice should be in front of the planners of every evangelism program. Planning may produce very little in any given generation, but Christians are learning, and the church as a whole is learning. When the church begins to understand the comprehensive nature of the gospel, and also the comprehensive nature of the church's responsibilities, and when all the assets of the church as a body can be tapped and applied by the various branches, then and only then can we and should we legitimately expect comprehensive, sustained revival.

The Need for True Revival

Unless we see revival in terms of at least a century-long process, we will be planning for a false revival. We will be planning for short-lived ecstatic outbreaks that are followed by cynicism and generations of skepticism. We have had enough of these before in church history. We do not need another one.

A revival should be a sharp and unexpected breaking into history by God's Spirit which subsequently blends into an extended period of institutional transformation. The revival should launch the process of transformation, but the subsequent social transformation is to be a direct heir of the revival itself. The discontinuity of revival must be followed by the continuity of social transformation, or else the revival is undermined.

Years of Preparation

What should a true revival look like? It should be preceded

by years of prayer and diligent work. Christians must prepare themselves for competent service. Then a sharp historical discontinuity occurs: the movement of the Holy Spirit. The Spirit brings justification (the legal declaration of "not guilty!") to millions of people, and gives them the moral righteousness of Christ: definitive sanctification. This sharp discontinuity into history and into the lives of newly regenerate people should then be followed by lives of personal continuity (progressive personal sanctification) and generations of social continuity: progressive cultural sanctification. Thus, the pattern is *continuity, discontinuity, continuity.* (This is point five of the biblical covenant model.)

What I am saying, then, is that the discontinuity of revival follows a long period of preparation, and is followed by an even longer period of social application. Revivals take place within history. Today, we see the technological tools in front of us, both for bringing the revival into homes where evangelical visitors seldom enter (ghettos, isolated villages), and for extending the initial transforming work of the revival for decades thereafter.

We need to see the work of revival lasting for a minimum of two generations, and probably more, just to transform the West. The transition from revival to reconstruction will be a continuous process, and reconstruction will take generations. The goal should be to have revival produce reconstruction in one region, and then have that reconstruction process help finance the next phase of the revival elsewhere.

To revive means to bring life back. It means to come back from the dead. It is God's pre-resurrection resurrection. A church which requires an annual revival is in desperate shape. First, revival will not come in response to a hired parachurch ministry which specializes in whooping up the troops for five evenings in a row once a year. The troops need boot camp more than they need a pep rally. They need an armory more than they need a nursery. They need meat more than they need milk. The church needs vision, motivation, and discipline.

Second, revival is what the lost need, not what the church

needs. While the lost may be in the churches, and while many denominations are lost, the church, as a church, is not in need of revival, for God's people have already been in principle resurrected. Their revival *was*. Their definitive sanctification *was*. Now they have to apply it: progressive sanctification. For that, they do not need revival. Instead, they need an awareness of the covenant.

A Stolen Vision

We can see how the biblical process of "continuity, discontinuity, continuity" is supposed to work by considering a specific case in American history when it failed to work. There was continuity and discontinuity, but the subsequent continuity was cut short.

In the decades prior to the Civil War (1861-65), the second Great Awakening, which began around 1800 and accelerated rapidly in the 1820-1850 period, brought many tens of thousands of people to a profession of faith in Jesus Christ, especially in the North and Midwest (then called the Northwest). (The First Great Awakening was the revival a century earlier, 1735-55, whose most famous preachers were the roving English evangelist George Whitefield [WHITfield] and pastor Jonathan Edwards, whose sermon, "Sinners in the Hands of an Angry God," with its unforgettable image of the spider suspended on a thread above the burning coals, may be the most famous sermon in American history.) Many of the evangelical leaders of the Great Awakening in the North became social activists, campaigning publicly against the institution of chattel slavery. The continuity of evangelism (1800-1820) brought on a religious discontinuity (the Second Great Awakening, 1820-50), which in turn helped bring a great political discontinuity: the Civil War.

But the God-required continuity after 1865 did not appear. After the war, this evangelical enthusiasm for social reform waned in Bible-believing circles. The revivalists from the beginning of the abolitionist movement had deferred to the intellectual leadership of liberal and radical Unitarians in New England, so the evangelicals never gained social and intellectual leadership in this reform effort. Abolitionism was a "common-ground" effort in which the New England radicals used the Christians as their "shock troops" in what became a revolutionary humanistic campaign to transform Christian America into a secular humanist country. (This is the inevitable danger of any co-operative reform effort between Christian activists and non-Christian activists, no matter how righteous the cause. If the Christians do not control most of the movement's leadership *and most of its money*, they should not co-operate. Christians must never allow themselves to become the tail on some other religious group's organizational dog.)

Theological liberals after 1865 secularized the evangelicals' pre-war social optimism, converting the Christians' vision of earthly victory and the building of the kingdom of God on earth socially and institutionally into a vision of victory of the kingdom of autonomous man on earth, a kingdom to be established primarily through political action. Thus, the discontinuity of the Second Great Awakening did not produce a continuity of Christian social reform and institution-building after 1865. The revival's discontinuity did not produce the kingdom's institutional continuity.

What followed was a theological war between liberalism and a new version of revivalism, 1865-1975, with the evangelicals more and more placing their hope in a *future discontinuous event* — the bodily Second Coming of Christ — to take them out of this continuously evil world. Thus, Bible-believing Christianity in the United States steadily lost its original faith in the earthly success of the church and the transforming power of the gospel prior to Christ's bodily return in glory. Christians lost faith in historical continuity. They placed their hopes and dreams of kingdom-building in a future beyond the day-to-day continuities of the Christian's daily moral walk with Christ. They saw the building of the kingdom of God on earth as the product solely of a great discontinuous future event, one completely outside their power to influence except (maybe) through personal soul-winning. "When that last person is brought to Christ, then He shall appear in the heavens!" Soul-winning became the focus of concern; social reform

became at most a downtown rescue mission operation to sober up
a few drunks, or a foreign orphanage operation, which all too often
imparted only the ability to read to young people, whereupon the
Communists recruited them because the Communists, rather than
the Christians, had produced a large quantity of literature that
promoted a deeply religious (atheist) vision of earthly victory.

At the same time that the evangelicals were adopting a
worldview based on historical discontinuity, the theological and
political liberals became the advocates of historical continuity.
They successfully stole the Christians' original vision of earthly
victory, and secularized it. (This successful theft is the source of
the myth still found in church history books that "postmillennial
social optimism is a form of theological liberalism." Why, then,
was virtually the entire faculty of Princeton Theological Seminary,
the nation's most prestigious Bible-believing seminary in the nineteenth and early twentieth century, both postmillennial and politically conservative throughout the nineteenth century? Why was
Princeton's Charles Hodge, a postmillennialist and author of the
famous *Systematic Theology*, the great opponent of Charles Darwin
and evolution?)

The Scopes Trial

This self-imposed cultural burial of Christians accelerated in
1925 with the Scopes "monkey trial" (evolution in the public
schools) and did not begin to change until the late 1970's, with the
appearance of the anti-abortion movement and the Presidential
candidacy of Southern Baptist Jimmy Carter. With the coming of
these preliminary signs of "salt and light revival" among fundamentalist Christians has also come the growth of doubt regarding
the prevailing eschatologies of earthly despair and Christian cultural retreat. What people believe inevitably affects what they do,
but what people do also affects what they believe.

Quite frankly, one reason why Christians today read and
believe David Chilton's little book, *The Great Tribulation* (Dominion
Press, 1987), which argues the commonly held pre-1900 theologi-

cal view that the great tribulation took place in 70 A.D. with the fall of Jerusalem to the Roman army, is because of the coming of the growing conflict over abortion. If Chilton is correct, this means that Christians' socially paralyzing concern over some inevitable catastrophe in the future — or the church's inevitable removal from history just before this inevitable catastrophe — is misplaced. It means that Christians need not fear the supposedly inevitable defeat of the gospel of Jesus Christ prior to His Second Coming in final judgment. It means, in short, that the church is not a loser in history. Therefore, our efforts as Christians to make the world better before Jesus returns to earth in glory are not doomed to inevitable defeat by Bible prophecy. Christians can lose many battles but not the war. As with any army, we can experience painful defeats, but the victory of our righteous cause is assured.

People do not want to join a personally risky battle that their leaders say cannot be won before Jesus comes to rapture them to the safety of heaven. Christian leaders who seek to mobilize followers in such confrontations have begun to abandon their former commitment to eschatologies of earthly defeat, especially the younger leaders. This is why the battle over abortion has led to a battle over eschatology. This is also why those fundamentalists who preached the older, culturally defeatist eschatologies did not immediately start protesting abortion after *Roe v. Wade* in 1973. The abortion issue has polarized Christians in many areas and for many reasons. The old rule is true: "You cannot change just one thing."

Conclusion

We must preach Christ and Him crucified. But we must also preach Christ resurrected and ascended, seated on the right hand of God in full authority. We must preach the Holy Spirit, God's representative who guides His people into all truth. We must preach the transcendence of God on high and the presence of God in our hearts and in our midst. Nothing less than this will do.

Christians need to challenge the lies and evils of our day — personal lies and evils, but also institutional lies and evils. Both challenges are important. To ignore either is to ignore God's offer of comprehensive redemption from sin. This inevitably means confrontation. It did in the early church, and it has ever since. Rome did not want to abandon the worship of the state. Neither does the modern world.

The decision of Christians to confront the institutional evils of their day is a prelude and handmaiden to revival. Without this willingness to become confrontational, God need not take us seriously. If we do not want comprehensive revival, we may not get even "soul-winning" revival. In the 1820's through the 1850's, the revivals of the Second Great Awakening were closely associated with the political and legal protest against the institutionalized evil of chattel slavery. Today, the protest against abortion seems to be the visible sign of Christian revival. If Christians fail to take this opportunity to challenge known evil, will this generation perish in the wilderness?

In summary:

1. To raise the question of obedience to unjust laws is to raise the question of social ethics.

2. We must ask ourselves: To what extent are we bound by sinful laws?

3. We must ask: By what right do unjust men rule over us?

4. We begin our search for answers with a consideration of the nature of God.

5. God is both transcendent and present.

6. God is wholly personal.

7. He is the Creator

8. His universe is therefore wholly personal.

9. He claims absolute sovereignty.

10. Covenant-breaking people deny this claim.

11. There is a war on between rival views of authority.

12. This war is political as well as theological.

13. The god of a society is its source of civil law.

14. This law will reflect the ethics of the god.

15. God is the only true source of law in society.

16. Christians deny the false gods of men and therefore the false legal orders that testify to such false gods.

17. Christians are therefore implicitly revolutionaries against all non-Christian social and legal orders.

18. Christians are in principle at war with much of society.

19. Christians want peace, but find themselves at war.

20. The comprehensive nature of Christ's claims forces them into a confrontation with anti-Christian societies.

21. Sin is comprehensive; therefore, the gospel's healing power is equally comprehensive.

22. God promises to bring healing to society in history.

23. Jesus fulfilled the Jubilee Year.

24. This jubilee has been proclaimed to the Gentiles.

25. God's covenant now extends to all nations.

26. The Holy Spirit empowers Christians to obey and extend this covenant.

27. Christians lack confidence because they do not understand how transcendent God is and how present He is.

28. Christians have been on the defensive.

29. God is not *judicially* absent.

30. The Gospel is confrontational.

31. Christians should think in terms of extending Christ's kingdom (civilization) in history before the Rapture.

32. We need revival: continuity, discontinuity, and continuity.

33. Christians need to challenge all the evils of our day.

2

THE VOICE OF LAWFUL AUTHORITY

Let every soul be subject unto the higher powers. For there is no power but of God: the powers that be are ordained of God. Whosoever therefore resisteth the power, resisteth the ordinance of God: and they that resist shall receive to themselves damnation (Romans 13:1-2).

Then went the captain with the officers, and brought them without violence: for they feared the people, lest they should have been stoned. And when they had brought them, they set them before the council: and the high court asked them, Saying, Did not we straitly command thee that ye should not teach in this name? And, behold, ye have filled Jerusalem with your doctrine, and intend to bring this man's blood upon us. Then Peter and the other apostles answered and said, We ought to obey God rather than men (Acts 5:26-29).

The apostles resisted the official demand of the religious authorities and the civil authorities to cease and desist from preaching in the name of Jesus, a convicted criminal. There is no doubt that this demand was as just as the conviction of Jesus in the Jewish and Roman courts – or as unjust.

Since the apostles resisted lawful authorities, were they in violation of Romans 13? If not, then how can we reconcile this apparent contradiction. Both of these passages are in the Bible. The Bible is the very Word of God, perfect and authoritative. It tells us what we are supposed to believe and do. All people are required by God to obey the Bible, His revealed Word, but espe-

40

cially Christians. This means that Christians must acknowledge, affirm, and obey the principles found in both passages. This is the Bible talking!

Why should Christians be more bound by the Bible than anyone else? Doesn't God hold all people responsible for their actions? He does, but Christians are even more responsible. The Bible teaches that from him who has been given much, much is required (Luke 12:48-49). Furthermore, Christians have pledged eternal obedience to Jesus Christ, their King, the incarnate Second Person of the Trinity. They have been baptized in His name, and therefore they are legally under His jurisdiction. *This, in fact, is the primary meaning of baptism: to place oneself under the judicial authority of God.* When someone has been baptized in the name of the Father, the Son, and the Holy Ghost, he or she has become God's man or God's woman. Once this mark of God's authority and man's subordination has been placed on a person, there can be no legal escape.

There are five things that we can say confidently about God's relationship to Christians over us: 1) God's Word is binding, 2) God's covenant authority is binding, 3) the covenant's laws are binding, 4) the sanctions (blessings and cursings) attached to this covenant are binding, 5) the sanctions are forever. We dare not forget or neglect even one of these five covenant principles. All five are binding on us, and God will hold us eternally accountable for believing and obeying all five.

This book does not attempt to set forth the case for the Bible as God's inspired Word. The book assumes this about the Bible, however. We begin with the second question: the lawful voice of authority. This is the question of *representation.* Which voice in history speaks authoritatively in the name of the God of the Bible? The Bible teaches that several authorities do: civil rulers, church rulers, family rulers, and the conscience. All four are God's lawful covenantal agents. All four have taken binding oaths, either explicitly or implicitly. Rulers swear to uphold the law: state, church, or family law. So does each individual. Men either accept Jesus

Christ as Lord-Savior, or they do not. A decision to reject Him is still a decision. In this case, *no decision is a decision*: a decision *against* Christ. It may be an implicit decision, but it is still legally binding, for in Adam, we have already sinned. In Adam, we all explicitly said "no" to God, *Adam was our lawful covenantal representative.* As mentioned earlier, the meaning of individual baptism is the affirmation of the legally binding nature of God's covenant. Thus, the individual Christian's conscience is a lawful voice of authority.

The Bible teaches that there is only one absolutely sovereign authority: God. There is only one absolutely sovereign voice of authority: the Bible. It is the responsibility of each subordinately sovereign lawful authority to conform himself to these two ultimate sovereigns. But civil authorities in history have rarely been willing to do this. The result has been injustice, generation after generation.

The Universal Dilemma of
Conflicting Lawful Authorities

Every society and every organization in man's history has faced the same sort of dilemma that Christians see in Romans 13:1-2 and Acts 5:26-29. Every society and every organization needs stability in order to function properly. This means that there must be a lawful chain of command in every organization. There must be a *hierarchy*. Someone is always held responsible by someone else above him. There is no escape from hierarchy. The only questions are: Who runs it? Who issues the orders in what ultimate sovereign's name? Who enforces the organization's rules?

This means inescapably that every organization is under the authority of someone or some group of people who will, from time to time, do evil things or ask their subordinates to do evil things. Men are sinners. Thus, the subordinate in any organization will eventually come to a crisis. Should he obey his superior when his superior tells him to do something that the subordinate regards as morally or legally wrong? Or should the subordinate listen to his conscience? This raises another question: By which voice is

God speaking to the person? Through his own conscience or through the voice of his superior? Soldiers in battle face these decisions. Middle management people in business face it. Bureaucrats in government organizations face it. It is not confined to Christians, and it is not confined to civil government. The question is: Who best represents God's moral will in any given situation?

The answer is difficult to determine. Good men will argue about the answer. They even argue about how to find the answer. But the fact remains: in history, men face this sort of decision all over the world. It is a familiar problem throughout history and in every society. It is the question of lawful authority and lawful obedience.

Normally, people believe that mutiny is wrong, especially during wartime. We all agree that a military commander in battle must be obeyed. Lives of other people depend on the faithful obedience of a commander's subordinates. Yet the legal authorization of mutiny — indeed, the legal obligation of subordinates to mutiny — was affirmed by modern humanist international law during the Nuremburg trials of German military leaders following World War II. The legal right to answer to the court, "I was just following orders," was removed from all defendants. High military officials were sentenced to death and executed by this international tribunal for their having failed to mutiny against Hitler and the German high command. This has been called "victor's justice," but it is now the legal precedent that military officers face. (This prededent may make it difficult for future wars to be settled peaceably short of the unconditional surrender of one side. Leaders of the losing side may decide they have nothing to lose by continuing the war, hoping for a miraculous turn of events.) Thus, there is no escape today from the dilemma of moral choice. Therefore, even in this seemingly obvious case — the question of military mutiny — civil courts present citizens with the same two seemingly opposed legal and moral standards that we find in Romans 13 and Acts 5.

Yet these standards are not in principle opposed. The Bible is true. God's Word is not inconsistent. Both principles are true: obey lawful authorities (plural, the text indicates) and obey God rather than man. Similarly, a chain of military command needs both rules: obedience to commanders, yet also the right of subordinates to disobey unlawful or immoral orders. In fact, an army that did not allow wide discretion to its subordinate officers and troops would be paralyzed; the general and his staff would have to know everything perfectly in order for them to issue absolutely binding orders. No army that required absolute obedience could win a war. There always has to be discretion down the chain of command. The sergeant who is told by the lieutenant, "Take your men up the front of that hill and capture it," may discover on the battlefield that he cannot obey this two-part order. He may believe that his men are able to capture the hill, but not if they go up the front. He has to make a quick decision here: Which is the more fundamental order, capturing the hill or going up its front? Most of us would assume that unless we were explicitly told otherwise, the senior commander wants to capture the hill, not see his troops get slaughtered by dutifully going up the front. The sergeant acts accordingly. He may be court-martialed later, but to get himself court-martialed, he first has to come back alive. Better to come back alive, preferably after having captured the hill.

This brings us to one of the most important laws of military justice: *there are few things better than a victory on the battlefield if you want to avoid being court-martialed.* This rule of thumb also governs all other human courts of justice. Ours is a created world. We are all creatures. We cannot know things perfectly, in the way that God knows them. Thus, when we are issued an order from on high, meaning an order from a "higher-up," we have to ask ourselves: How should this order be obeyed? Furthermore, we must ask: Is there a higher order from someone even higher up the chain of command? In short, *Is my commander being obedient to the orders he received from his commander?*

Let us never forget: *the highest commander of all is God.*

The Doctrine of Interposition

Christians must protest against injustice. This is basic to evangelism. If we preach against sin, then we must preach against injustice. But how is this to be done biblically? It must be done *representatively*. The Christian who gets involved in an organized protest against civil injustice is acting as a *covenantal agent* on someone else's behalf. He is interposing himself and his associates in between a corrupt civil government and its innocent victims. This is why we say that he is acting *representatively*. Thus, before a Christian joins such a protest or movement, he should have some idea about the biblical doctrine of representation. This doctrine, if properly understood, leads to another doctrine, the doctrine of *interposition*. The biblical doctrine of representation begins with the concept of the covenant, the foundation of all lawful government.

It should be obvious that the most important representative agent in man's history was Jesus Christ, who interposed Himself in between God the Father and rebellious humanity. Without this interposition, there would never have been history. On the day that Adam sinned, God would have killed him, body and soul. It is only because God looked forward in history to Jesus Christ's act of interposition that He spared the family of man. This was an interposition of grace between God's sovereign justice and judicially guilty mankind, for man deserved to die. *Jesus Christ interposed Himself judicially and physically.* How much more should Christians become involved in interposition between injustice and judicially innocent victims!

Before we consider in greater detail the biblical doctrine of interposition, we need to understand the concept of covenantal government. Such government is always hierarchical. Once we understand how covenantal government operates, we can then discuss on what basis an individual can interpose himself, *judicially and physically*, in between unjust government and its judicially innocent victims.

Self-Government Directly Under God

Each person is responsible before God for everything he says and does in his lifetime. Jesus warned us: "But I say unto you, That every idle word that men shall speak, they shall give account thereof in the day of judgment" (Matthew 12:36). Thus, a person's conscience is a lawful authority. The fundamental rule of government is *self-government under God's law*. The primary enforcing agent is the conscience. No other human government possesses the God-given authority or the God-given resources to police every aspect of each person's daily walk before God. Any government that attempts this is inherently tyrannical.

When a person faces God on judgment day, there will be no committee beside him to "take the rap." Only Jesus Christ can do this for a person, as God's lawful authorized authority who died in place of a God-redeemed individual. There will be no one else except Jesus Christ at the throne of judgment who can lawfully intervene and tell God the Judge, "This person was following my orders, and therefore should not be prosecuted."

Therefore, the fundamental *representative* voice of God's authority in each person's life is his own conscience. Because the individual will face God on judgment day, the fundamental form of human government is self-government. This is basic to Christian ethical, social, and legal theory. Any society that attempts to deny this principle of justice is in revolt against God.

This is not to say that a person's conscience is absolutely sovereign. There has been no single, God-authorized human voice of absolute authority on earth since the ascension of Jesus Christ to the right hand of God. The conscience is a person's primary voice of authority, but a wise person will defer to other God-ordained human authorities. The Bible is clear about this. *There is a division of labor in every area of life, including the proper interpreting of God's law.* The church of Jesus Christ is a body with many members (Romans 12; I Corinthians 12). Paul in Ephesians writes:

And he gave some, apostles; and some, prophets; and some, evangelists; and some, pastors and teachers; For the perfecting of the saints, for the work of the ministry, for the edifying of the body of Christ: Till we all come in the unity of the faith, and of the knowledge of the Son of God, unto a perfect man, unto the measure of the stature of the fulness of Christ: That we henceforth be no more children, tossed to and fro, and carried about with every wind of doctrine, by the sleight of men, and cunning craftiness, whereby they lie in wait to deceive; But speaking the truth in love, may grow up into him in all things, which is the head, even Christ: From whom the whole body fitly joined together and compacted by that which every joint supplieth, according to the effectual working in the measure of every part, maketh increase of the body unto the edifying of itself in love (Ephesians 4:11-16).

We are told that "Where no counsel is, the people fall: but in the multitude of counsellors there is safety" (Proverbs 11:14). Thus, *no person's conscience is autonomous.* (Auto = self; nomos = law.) The conscience is the primary authority under God because any act of rebellion against God by a person's conscience will be held against that person in God's perfect court of justice. It is not the sole authority under God.

Are consciences reliable? We are told by Paul: "For when the Gentiles, which have not the law, do by nature the things contained in the law, these, having not the law, are a law unto themselves. Which shew the work of the law written in their hearts, their conscience also bearing witness. . ." (Romans 2:14-15a). Understand, the law of God is not said to be written on their hearts; only the *work* of the law is written there. It is only regenerate people who have the law of God itself written on their hearts (Hebrews 8:9-10; 10:16). Nevertheless, the work of the law testifies against all men when they rebel against God's law. They know better. The redeemed person in principle knows best, but the unregenerate at least knows better when he sins.

The human conscience is not perfect in its transmission of God's warnings. Its signals can be ignored by a person for so long that he or she no longer responds. Paul calls this a *seared conscience*: "Now the Spirit speaketh expressly, that in the latter times some shall depart from the faith, giving heed to seducing spirits, and doctrines of devils; speaking lies in hypocrisy; having their conscience seared with a hot iron" (I Timothy 4:1-2).

Christians do not take these words literally, of course. We do not believe that a literal hot iron can sear a person's conscience. Paul was using a metaphor. A bleeding wound can be sealed up by applying a hot iron to it, but the nerve endings beneath the skin may be permanently destroyed. The person later may lose all feeling on the seared portion of his flesh. So it is with sin. If false doctrines or evil acts are indulged in, they can sear the conscience. No longer will the individual hear the warning voice of God. Again, this is not a literal voice. The conscience is *representatively* the voice of God, but it is nonetheless conscience, not literally a voice.

Self-Government Under Church Authority

God has ordained the church as His lawful monopoly that governs the distribution (and therefore the withholding) of the sacraments. Like any God-ordained sovereign government, the church is run hierarchically. There is a chain of command. This is not a top-down bureaucratic chain of command. God has established a system of multiple bottom-up appeals courts: church, state, and family. This appeals court structure is seen in the civil government's court procedure described in Exodus 18 and also in the church government's court procedure described in Matthew 18:15-18.

In contrast to God's appeals court hierarchy, Satan runs a top-down chain of command. In a bureaucracy, the leader issues orders that must be obeyed. He runs the bureaucracy the way a general runs an army during a war. But a general during a war is made personally responsible for the success or failure of the life-and-death military operations. This level of personal responsibility does not prevail in peacetime, when civilian rule again becomes the standard. Also, the focus of a war is narrow: military victory. This concentration of national and personal focus is narrow, unlike a peacetime society. Thus, a bureaucratic approach to institutional rule is suitable temporarily during a war, but it is not the organizational standard in a free society when each person is made personally responsible for fulfilling God's command to subdue the earth (Genesis 1:26-28). Bureaucracy cannot make full use of the division of labor principle except when the assigned task of the organization is very narrow and universally accepted by a large majority of citizens.

Satan is not all-seeing or all-powerful, so he has to issue commands to a massive bureaucracy of both human and demonic followers. Yet even he cannot issue perfect commands; even he has to allow for some latitude in his subordinates' literal obedience. He is a creature. He seeks to compensate for his lack of omniscience by strengthening the power of his bureaucracy.

Church government, like family government and civil government, is always hierarchical. There are officers in a church: deacons and elders. They have to meet exacting moral and family discipline requirements in order to serve as officers (I Timothy 3). Church officers are required to settle disputes that arise between church members (I Corinthians 6). But the appeals usually arise from below. The leaders of the church, being voluntary (in contrast to minor children in a family) must lead by example. They do not issue commands, except when formally deciding a case brought to them. They announce God's law from the pulpit. The church can lawfully initiate a covenant lawsuit against rebellious members, but a church that does this continually will not hold its members. Cults are marked by continual top-down monitoring; churches are marked by self-government under God's law.

Churches are sometimes organized as independent congregations. Rare is the local church, however, that is not connected in some way to an association of other churches with similar beliefs. Sometimes churches are organized hierarchically as denominations, that is, hierarchically. The chain of command is formal. Higher governmental bodies are allowed to impose discipline on individuals through the subordinate authority of their local churches. But there can be no church apart from some sort of hierarchical discipline, any more than there can be an army without hierarchical discipline.

Which Church to Join?

This is why an individual should not join a church whose judicial authority he does not trust. When he joins, he places himself under this authority. He is required to join in order to take communion, a God-ordained, God-required sacrament. The church's final official act of discipline is excommunication: separation from (ex = out of) communion. Thus, every Christian is required by God to belong to a church, for without membership there can be no discipline; without discipline, there can be no "army of the Lord" and no government. The conscience is not a sufficient voice of authority. There must be a multitude of counsellors (Proverbs 11:14).

A person must decide, through the testimony of his conscience, which doctrines and practices are most important on God's hierarchy of values, and he must then join that church which adheres most closely to this set of values. This is not a denial of conscience; it is an affirmation of conscience. The conscience is a person's representative voice of God when he chooses which church to join. After joining, he transfers some of this authority over his conscience to the church government and away from self-government, in much the same way that a woman transfers a degree of authority over her conscience from her father to her husband when she marries. *She* does this. She makes this decision under God. Marriage is not a denial of her rights of conscience but rather an affirmation of these rights. Similarly, colonial Americans transferred varying degrees of sovereignty to the national civil government in 1788 when they ratified the U.S. Constitution. They did not abdicate their consciences, but they did abdicate any pretensions of possessing autonomous consciences.

In order to affirm the rights of conscience, God tells us to choose which church we will obey. He brings us under authority, but not apart from our individual consciences. If we find that we have made a bad choice, and the church we selected is in fact not obeying God the way we believe it should, then we may transfer membership. We may not become autonomous, for this is a denial of God's law. We are told by God to join a church, but we must allow our conscience to be our guide, under the overall authority of God's Spirit and God's revealed Word, the Bible.

Self-Government Under Civil Authority

The ultimate lawful authority to inflict physical and all other sanctions belongs to God. "Vengeance is mine; I will repay, saith the Lord" (Romans 12:19b). He delegates this authority to families over young children and to civil governments. Romans 13 makes it clear that an individual is always under some form of civil authority. The civil magistrate is actually called "the minister of God" (verse 4). The minister of civil justice possesses lawful authority to impose physical punishments on those under the state's jurisdiction. Individuals are not to inflict corporal punishment on others, except in the case of parents punishing their minor children, and schoolteachers or other parent-designated authorities who do the same as lawful representatives of the parents.

Renouncing State Jurisdiction

The Bible therefore teaches that men are under the lawful authority of one or more civil governments. As in church government, this judicial authority is supposed to be enforced hierarchically, on an appeals-court basis. The civil law is given to men by God through the state in order to establish boundaries of lawful individual and corporate behavior. The biblical legal principle is this: "Whatever is not forbidden is allowed." Like Adam in the garden, who could lawfully eat from any of the trees in the garden except one, so is man allowed by civil law to do anything he wants that is not explicitly prohibited in the Bible or implicitly prohibited by the application of a biblical principle. Civil government, like church government, imposes restraints on evil behavior; its role is to keep men from doing evil acts, not to make men good. It is supposed to impose negative sanctions against evil behavior. *The state is not an agency of personal salvation.* It is not supposed to save men; it is to protect them from the evil acts of other men.

The individual is supposed to possess the God-given legal right to remove himself from the jurisdiction of any civil government that he believes to be immoral. Because civil governments rule over geographical areas, the act of renouncing jurisdiction is normally accomplished through personal emigration. Until World War I, the right of legal emigration out of a nation and almost universal immigration into a nation were honored in Europe and North America. Very few nations required passports.

Because of the difficulty of moving, especially prior to the invention of the steam engine (ships and trains), God has established other means of renouncing jurisdiction. One of these is the right of revolution. This right is lawful only when conducted by lesser magistrates who have been raised up by God to challenge immoral rulers. The Book of Judges deals with this right of revolution by lesser magistrates and national leaders who revolt against foreign invaders who have established long-term rule.

Legitimate Deception of Unjust Rulers

Another of these God-given alternatives to departing physically is the right of civil disobedience. Men refuse to obey unjust laws. The obvious biblical example of this is the revolt of the Hebrew midwives against Pharaoh. They refused to carry out his order to kill all the male babies. They lied to him about the extra-rapid delivery of Hebrew women (Ex. 1:19), a lie so obviously preposterous that only a man blinded by God could have believed it. After all, if the wives were delivered so rapidly, of what possible use could a midwife be? There could be no such thing as a midwife. Then God blessed them in this act of rebellion (Ex. 1:20).

Notice that they did not inquire with any civil magistrate regarding the lawfulness of their acts of defiance. There is no indication that they checked with the elders of Israel. They simply began to resist the murderous plans of the Pharaoh with the only tool available to them: lying. *There was no biblical requirement that they gain formal public support from a lower magistrate, since they were not taking up arms against the state.* They were not violent in any way against lawful authority. They resisted peacefully, so they did not need the approval of any civil magistrate.

Similar acts of civil disobedience – acts of treason, in fact – were committed by Rahab. First, she committed treason by covenanting to the God of Israel through the spies. Ultimately, whenever a Christian covenants with God, he has committed an act of treason against "the powers that be," unless Christians are these powers. Second, she hid the Hebrew spies. Third, she sent them on their way. Fourth, she remained behind, under the geographical juris-diction of the city of Jericho, in order to fool the rulers. Fifth, she lied to the Jericho authorities about their whereabouts (Joshua 2). God then blessed her. Her whole family survived the fall of Jericho. In fact, she actually became part of the Davidic line, and her name is mentioned in Matthew's genealogy of Jesus (Matthew 1:5).

These very acts of obeying God made them outlaws, if by law we mean the law of the civil governments that they were under. Because of the nature of the public rebellion of the civil rulers against God, treason against the government was obedience to God.

The Hebrew midwives and Rahab took grave risks. They might have been executed. This risk was inescapable, given the nature of their deception. To have fled would have been either impossible (the midwives in Egypt) or self-defeating (Rahab's subsequent deception of the rulers). This raises a very important point that must be understood very clearly before anyone chooses to involve himself in similar acts of civil disobedience. *These women placed themselves under the threat of external civil sanctions. This was the price of a successful rebellion.* To have avoided these risks, they would have had to flee. Their unwillingness to flee placed them under the rebellious state's sanctions. They might have been executed. But they faced this danger without visible flinching. In fact, their courage must have been part of the success of their plan of civil disobedience. Had they shown fear, their lies might have been detected. Only because they did not show fear did the rulers accept their lies as true.

The Biblical Justification for Lying

The Bible says that Christians should not lie to each other. "Wherefore putting away lying, speak every man truth with his neighbour: for we are members one of another" (Ephesians 4:25). But this rule does not always prevail in dealings between civil governments or between governments and their citizens. For example, civil governments certainly believe in the legitimacy of military lying, so they train and send out spies, and they camouflage troops and weapons. Moses sent spies into Canaan before the invasion (Numbers 14). Joshua, who had been one of the spies under Moses, did the same a generation later (Joshua 2). Are we to say such decisions by civil governments are morally wrong? If so, then why did God allow Moses and Joshua to send out spies to spy out the land of Canaan? In times such as today — days filled with life-and-death crises — Christians had better not be naive about such matters. If Christians are morally required by God to avoid lying to the civil government in all cases, then on what moral basis did Christians in Europe hide Jews in their homes during the terror of the Nazis?

If you have qualms about accepting the idea of self-conscious lying as a legitimate part of civil disobedience, please consider the following passages in the Bible to see how God deliberately lies to unjust civil rulers and false prophets in order to bring them low:

> And the LORD said, Who shall persuade Ahab, that he may go up and fall at Ramoth-gilead? And one said on this manner, and another said on that manner. And there came forth a spirit, and stood before the LORD, and said, I will persuade him. And the LORD said unto him, Wherewith? And he said, I will go forth, and I will be a lying spirit in the mouth of all his prophets. And he said,

Thou shalt persuade him, and prevail also: go forth, and do so. Now therefore, behold, the LORD hath put a lying spirit in the mouth of all these thy prophets, and the LORD hath spoken evil concerning thee (I Kings 22:20-23).

For every one of the house of Israel, or of the stranger that sojourneth in Israel, which separateth himself from me, and setteth up his idols in his heart, and putteth the stumblingblock of his iniquity before his face, and cometh to a prophet to inquire of him concerning me; I the LORD will answer him by myself: And I will set my face against that man, and will make him a sign and a proverb, and I will cut him off from the midst of my people; and ye shall know that I am the LORD. And if the prophet be deceived when he hath spoken a thing, I the LORD have deceived that prophet, and I will stretch out my hand upon him, and will destroy him from the midst of my people Israel. And they shall bear the punishment of their iniquity: the punishment of the prophet shall be even as the punishment of him that seeketh unto him (Ezekiel 14:7-10).

The relevant New Testament passage is II Thessalonians 2:11-12: "And for this cause God shall send them strong delusion, that they should believe a lie: That they all might be damned who believed not the truth, but had pleasure in unrighteousness." Are we to say that we cannot do likewise under any circumstances? Are we supposed to be holier than God? People who try to be holier than God wind up like Satan: initially tyrannical and then impotent.

Another case in the Bible of someone who broke the law of the state was Jehosheba, who saved the life of the infant heir to the throne, Joash. "And when Athaliah the mother of Ahaziah saw that her son was dead, she arose and destroyed all the seed royal. But Jehosheba, the daughter of king Joram, sister of Ahaziah, took Joash the son of Ahaziah, and stole him from among the king's sons which were slain; and they hid him, even him and his nurse, in the bedchamber from Athaliah, so that he was not slain" (II Kings 11:1-2). By whose authority did she do this? By her own, under God. She took the baby to God's house, which served as a sanctuary for him until he came of age. "And he was with her hid

in the house of the LORD six years. And Athaliah did reign over
the land" (II Kings 11:3). There was no lower civil magistrate
involved here. The senior officer of the church took full responsibility for this revolt against civil authority.

Does Mightq Make Right?

God brought negative sanctions in history against Egypt and
Jericho. God also brought positive sanctions in history to the
midwives and Rahab. This proves that God's civil government
(the civil aspect of God's universal kingdom) is alone absolutely
sovereign, and earthly civil governments are hierarchically subordinate to God's kingdom rule. The civil government that imposes
final sanctions in history and eternity is the absolutely sovereign
civil government in history and eternity.

This does not mean that "might makes right." It means that
God is right, God is mighty, and the kings of the earth will bow
down to him. It was not the task of the midwives or Rahab to
attempt to force the kings of their day to bow down to God. They
were not required or authorized by God to bring visible negative
sanctions against these rebellious rulers. These women were not
civil rulers themselves; they had no legal authority to bring negative physical sanctions against those in office over them. Vengeance was God's, as it is today. But they were required by God to
act as law-abiding righteous people by lying to the rulers, confus-
ing them, and thwarting their proclamations. Then God brought
the rulers low.

When Paul was brought before the Roman council in Jerusalem, the room was filled with Jewish religious leaders, who were
in fact subordinate rulers to Roman civil authority. They had
already admitted this in public at the most judicially critical point
in Israel's history, the crucifixion of Christ the Messiah: "But they
cried out, Away with him, away with him, crucify him. Pilate saith
unto them, Shall I crucify your King? The chief priests answered,
We have no king but Caesar" (John 19:15).

The Jewish leaders were divided between Pharisees, who believed in the resurrection of the dead at judgment day, as the Old Testament taught (Dan. 12:1-3), while the Sadducees, who ruled the temple, rejected this doctrine. So, when Paul testified to the Roman authorities, he told them the truth, the partial truth, and everything but the whole truth. He announced that he was on trial because he was a Pharisee and believed in the resurrection. Yes, he was a Pharisee — by birth. Yes, he believed in the resurrection — first of Jesus Christ, then of Christians, and then the unbelievers (I Corinthians 15). This was hardly orthodox Pharisaical doctrine. But he neglected to mention these "minor" doctrinal qualifications. Immediately, the two Jewish factions began screaming against each other, and the meeting broke up (Acts 23:6-10). Thus, he escaped civil judgment that day.

The moral and legal dilemma arises when there is a conflict among these lawful voices of authority. One or more of these God-authorized voices of lawful authority may issue commands that are in conflict with God's Bible-revealed law. What is the Christian supposed to do?

Conclusion

We have seen that all covenantal government is hierarchical. Someone or some lawful agency must speak in the name of the god of that society or group. Biblically, men are required by God to speak only in His name, according to His revelation of Himself in the Bible and in history. Because rulers often refuse to acknowledge that God is above them, they refuse to speak God's name. They become representatives of another god.

This makes decisions far more complex for Christians. Should they obey God or the civil magistrate? They must obey God. But as in all other decisions in life, there are levels of importance in decision-making. Some issues are more important than others. The human conscience needs earthly counsel in sorting out God's *hierarchy of values* and the *hierarchy of assigned responsibilities* that God presents to each person, moment by moment. We cannot fight every evil, right every wrong. We are creatures. We have limits on our lives. Thus, we must seek out our own specialized areas of service to God, which includes our own specialized areas of resistance to rebellious authority. Different people will regard different service as "the first and foremost," which others will not see so clearly. People also learn. They change their minds. Christian activists must be patient with other Christians in these matters, especially regarding timing. We live in a world governed by the principle of the division of intellectual labor. Success in competition often tells us which tactic was best, but only after the fact. Tactical questions and strategic questions in wartime baffle the best of generals, and daily living is surely more complex than mere military conflict. So, patience is basic to successful Christian recruiting and mobilization — in evangelism surely, but also in Christian activism.

When an individual decides what his priorities are, meaning God's priorities in his life, he must act in accordance with his conscience. He must march forward. If a Christian lives in a pagan culture, then his long-term goal should be the undermining of the present order and its replacement with a righteous order. This is the biblical concept of the leaven principle (Matthew 13:33). Evil must be replaced by good. *You cannot beat something with nothing.* You must have a positive program.

We cannot fight every fight, right every wrong, or save every life. We must pick and choose our tactical confrontations in terms of an overall strategy. We may concentrate our limited resources on one city, one project, or one person. We do this because we believe in the biblical doctrine of representation. We understand the use of symbols. If we can hinder or stop a *representative evil* locally, we thereby give visible warning to our enemies and visible encouragement to our allies.

Choose your allies well. Most important, choose your leaders well. Do your best not to go into public confrontation with your family and church against you, as well as the state. Subordinate yourself to God through His lawful institutions. If your pastor and elders are opposed to what you are doing to challenge the state, it is time to start looking for a new church.

In summary:

1. Christians are called upon to obey the civil government (Romans 13:1-8), but also to disobey evil laws (Acts 5:29).

2. We are baptized into God's covenant.

3. The covenant's five principles are binding on us.

4. The question of the lawful voice of authority is the question of lawful representation.

5. Only God and the Bible are absolutely sovereign.

6. Every society needs a hierarchy.

7. The question is: Who runs it?

8. Every hierarchy will eventually ask people to do something immoral or illegal.

9. Who represents God in such a situation?

10. Men must obey lawful authorities (plural).

11. Orders usually have more than one goal.

12. Subordinates must determine which is more fundamental.

13. God is the supreme commander.

14. The Bible teaches the doctrine of judicial interposition.

15. This also can involve bodily interposition.

16. The crucifixion displayed both aspects.

17. Each person is directly responsible under God.

18. Each person will be judged individually by God at the final judgment.

19. The representative between God and man is the human conscience.

20. Each person is under God's direct authority.

21. His own conscience is his representative for God.

22. No conscience is autonomous.

23. The *work* of the law is written on all hearts (though not the law itself).

24. Some consciences are seared by evil.

25. God's church supplements the human conscience.

26. The church's hierarchy is a bottom-up appeals court.

27. Satan's bureaucracy is a top-down command system.

28. An individual must decide for himself which church is closest to God's hierarchy of values and requirements.

29. He must do the same with civil government.

30. God's rule is: Whatever is not forbidden is allowed.

31. People can lawfully protest a civil violation of God's law.

32. They can lawfully use deception as a means of circumventing a biblically immoral law.

33. Permission of lower magistrates is not required for non-violent resistance.

34. God is right, and He possesses absolute might.

35. Honest men disagree regarding God's hierarchy of values.

36. They disagree over tactics and timing.

37. This is inevitable in a division-of-labor world.

38. We should choose our allies in terms of our assessment of both principles and tactics.

III. Ethics/Law (dominion)

3

HONORING GOD'S LAW BY
DISOBEYING EVIL HUMANIST LAWS

And Pharaoh charged all his people, saying, Every son that is born ye shall cast into the river, and every daughter ye shall save alive. And there went a man of the house of Levi, and took to wife a daughter of Levi. And the woman conceived, and bare a son: and when she saw him that he was a goodly child, she hid him three months. And when she could not longer hide him, she took for him an ark of bulrushes, and daubed it with slime and with pitch, and put the child therein; and she laid it in the flags by the river's brink. And his sister stood afar off, to wit what would be done to him. And the daughter of Pharaoh came down to wash herself at the river; and her maidens walked along by the river's side; and when she saw the ark among the flags, she sent her maid to fetch it. And when she had opened it, she saw the child: and, behold, the babe wept. And she had compassion on him, and said, This is one of the Hebrews' children. (Exodus 1:22-2:6)

Here is a story about disobedience. The parents of Moses deliberately hid him from the authorities. Then they put him in the river, but not in the way that Pharaoh had wanted. They placed him in a tiny ark. Then Pharaoh's daughter found it. She knew what kind of baby this was: the forbidden kind, the kind that were supposed to be tossed into the river. Did she obey her father's law? No, she took the baby and raised it as her own.

Eighty years after she disobeyed her father, Moses led the people of God out of Egypt, having destroyed the bulk of Egyptian

61

society by calling down God's judgments on it.

Exodus begins with disobedience. An evil Pharaoh broke the earlier Pharaoh's covenant with Joseph and his family. He made slaves out of them. Then he tried to get the Hebrew midwives to kill the male children, a violation of God's law against murder (Genesis 9:5). Then he ordered the male infants to be drowned. At least some of the Hebrews refused to obey. Then Pharaoh's daughter disobeyed her father.

The Law of the Two Covenants

God's law has stipulations; so did Pharaoh's. The biblical covenant's stipulations are based on permanent moral principles; these in turn reflect the permanent moral character of God. "For I am the LORD, I change not; therefore ye sons of Jacob are not consumed" (Malachi 3:6). This verse tells us that the preservation of the covenant and the covenant people of God is based on God's unchanging character.

Specific judicial applications can change when a change in covenantal administration occurs, such as the abolition of animal sacrifices after Jesus Christ's once-for-all sacrifice (Hebrews 9). God has the prerogative to change the external stipulations and external sanctions when the covenant is renewed. Nevertheless, God tells us that He does not change. The changes in civil law are made for the sake of the vassals under the King's protection, not for the sake of the King's changing circumstances. As the vassals become more mature, the application of God's laws becomes increasingly rigorous, such as the case of the New Testament's tightening of the laws of monogamy and divorce (Matthew 5:31-32). (Those who argue that the New Covenant loosened the bonds of the Old Covenant law have trouble with these New Covenant standards.) Civil law moves forward through time just as all other forms of knowledge move forward.

The ancient kingdom of Persia attempted to create absolutely changeless law. When the king spoke, he could not take back his words. This is why Darius had to throw Daniel into the lions' den, even though he had changed his mind about the original law (Daniel 6). But these ancient kingdoms all fell. Their laws fell with them. Kings spoke supposedly unchanging words, but their words faded with their empires.

Legal Positivism and Evolution

In modern times, however, all this has changed. The hallmark of all law, ever since Darwin's concept of evolution through natural selection captured the minds of most intellectuals a century ago, is relativism. The law changes when the sovereign people change their minds, meaning when their true spokesmen, the law-makers and especially the judicial interpreters of the law, change their minds. Legal positivism teaches that law is what the state says it is.

The man who pioneered the evolutionary concept of Constitutional law in the United States was Oliver Wendell Holmes, Jr., who wrote *The Common Law* in 1881. He once offered this definition of civil law: "The prophecies of what the courts will do in fact, and nothing more pretentious. . . ." Civil law is reduced by Darwinism to little more than mere speculation about paper-thin decisions of the Supreme Court. Holmes served on the U.S. Supreme Court for over three decades. His fellow Supreme Court justice Benjamin Cardozo praised him as "the philosopher and seer, the greatest of our age in the domain of jurisprudence and one of the greatest of all ages." His life was immortalized — humanists believe — in the famous biography that public school 11th graders used to read, back when the level of public school literacy was higher: *The Yankee from Olympus.*

Undergirding the biblical concept of law is the doctrine of an all-knowing, perfectly just God who will bring all things to light on the day of final judgment. Biblical law is grounded in the objective fact of the Creator God who speaks the law, enforces His law in history, and will serve as Final Judge. Darwinian law in the United States is grounded on nothing more substantial than temporary 5 to 4 decisions of the U.S. Supreme Court. Former Chief

Justice Warren Burger was interviewed by Bill Moyers just after the former had announced his resignation from the Court. The exchange is quite revealing:

CHIEF JUSTICE BURGER: Constitutional cases — constitutional jurisprudence is open to the Court to change its position, in view of — of changing conditions. And it has done so.

MOYERS: And what does it take for the Court to reverse itself?

CHIEF JUSTICE BURGER: Five votes.

The U.S. Supreme Court has reversed itself over 150 times in its history. This is an extremely important fact for all those who are considering the legitimacy of non-violent public protests against some law. The so-called law of the land keeps changing. The Court responds to public pressures. It is subject to new appointments by the President. In short, the modern concept of law is wholly statist, divorced from any concept of permanent moral truth or even logical truth. The law is little more than a fluctuating majority of Supreme Court justices.

It is well known that law school professors train their students to get existing laws overturned by the courts. It is a prestigious thing to have been the lawyer who persuaded the Supreme Court to reverse itself. But these same professors speak to the general public in terms of the sacrosanct law of the land.

For a Darwinist, there is no such thing as "sacrosanct." There are only changing environmental conditions and social responses to those changing conditions. Thus, when a protester decides to take a stand for a different interpretation of the civil law, the consistent Darwinist has to say that this may be the dawn of a new era. Like the random genetic change that makes a particular member of a species "more fit" to survive in his changing environment, so is the citizen who protests an existing law. The Darwinist who remains true to his faith can have nothing critical to say about the morality of such protests and changes. He rejects the whole idea of a permanent moral code independent from changing external social and environmental conditions. Any protest could be the herald of the new age, the next evolutionary leap of being.

If the law of God's covenant reveals that a particular activity is both immoral and illegal by God's civil standards, then Christians must oppose this behavior. If the modern humanistic state refuses to prosecute or even subsidizes such behavior, then Christians are authorized by God to protest: politically, judicially, and in the court of public opinion. God's law sanctions every kind of protest, including violent revolution if lower magistrates approve. Such protests are to be governed by the tactical rule that the reaction by the public that is sought by the protestors should determine the action pursued, as well as by the strategic covenantal rule that no violence by individuals against the state is legitimate without the approval of a lower magistrate. The protesters should strive to be as the children of Issachar, possessing an understanding of their times: "And of the children of Issachar, which were men that had understanding of the times, to know what Israel ought to do; the heads of them were two hundred; and all their brethren were at their commandment" (I Chronicles 12:32).

Civil magistrates do not like this view of the lawfulness of public protests against them, but their worldview is grounded in Darwinism. They may not like what Christians do to protest, but they have no moral foundation from which to launch a principled protest of their own. They can only appeal to political power. Darwinism leads whole civilizations to commit moral suicide. That humanistic civil magistrates and bureaucrats have nothing to say in response to organized civil disobedience except that such activities are in violation of the existing law should surprise no one. This is an irrelevant response; the whole purpose of the protest is to get the existing law changed.

The modern humanist world is morally defenseless against its organized enemies. Humanism's justice operates strictly in terms of sentiment and power. This is the moral legacy of Darwinism. The very moral impotence of the modern power state makes it vulnerable to attacks on its integrity by principled opponents.

Confrontation: Morality vs. Power

The success in retrospect of the officially non-violent protests of Gandhi and Martin Luther King should not lure Christian protesters into a trap. Protests can get out of hand. Gandhi's did, and so did King's on occasion. King's initially non-violent activities led to a weakening of moral resolve on the part of white Northerners as well as white Southerners. The white South repented about as fast and as much as a society can; the North, in contrast, became guilt-ridden and highly vulnerable to the demands of black hustlers who were hiding under the cover of righteousness. Thus, the years 1965-68 brought violence and riots to the black ghettos of the North, but violence barely touched the South after the passage of the Civil Rights Act of 1964.

The lesson that must be learned from the experiences of previous non-violent protest movements is this: personal salvation is achieved solely by the absolutely sovereign grace of God through faith in the atoning work of Jesus Christ at Calvary. Corporate or social salvation (healing) is by means of external faithfulness to the terms of God's covenant law. The state is an instrument of justice, not salvation. It imposes negative sanctions against public evil acts. The state should not be expected to achieve anything more than the slow but steady reduction of public evil.

To place great confidence in the state is to deify it, to make it into a god, a "god by default" in the era of Darwinism. This god will surely fail. The thwarted messianic hopes and dreams of arsonist blacks and the counter-culture of the 1965-70 period produced explosions of violence in the United States, especially on the prestigious university campuses. The students had believed their humanist professors. They had become worshippers at the temple of politics. When all they got in return was dull bureaucracy and more promises from the campus authorities, they revolted. But the revolts failed. Students then got even more dull bureaucracy and fewer promises. By the fall of 1970 — the semester following the U.S. invasion of Cambodia and the National Guard's shooting of several students at Kent State University in Ohio — student protests disappeared. The counter culture disappeared from the campus in one summer. Bureaucracy had done what it always does: outlast the protests.

Nevertheless, the campus was never the same again. The old self-confidence of secular humanism was shattered. The "can-do" liberalism of the Kennedy-Johnson era died. Academic standards began a long, steady decline after 1964. They did not recover after 1970. The bureaucrats prevailed, but their triumph was not glorious. They merely retained the power to preside over the disintegration of the older humanism. The students had removed their sense of possessing the moral high ground. The protests of 1965-70 had not stripped the bureaucrats of their power, but they had stripped them of their self-esteem.

The Moral High Ground

When Christian protestors confront the state in the name of a higher morality, they should not expect to do much more than to reduce the most obvious of public moral evils. In fact, it is through non-violent protest, and especially through the oppressive, immoral, and nearly demonic reaction of the police and politicians, that the moral evil of a public policy is exposed to the general public. Only if the public is totally corrupt can this reaction fail to gain supporters. The authorities' over-reaction will also attract outraged supporters who then join the protests. The protest then benefits from the snowball effect. The authorities' brutality backfires.

Viewers can see the over-reaction by the authorities. This over-reaction points beyond the visible confrontation to the overall immorality of the authorities' cause. This in turn points to the focus of the protest. The immoral civil authorities are increasingly seen by the general public as villains; so are the evil people who are being protected by the authorities. The general public, usually indifferent, can be aroused. The primary political objective of the tactics of Christian covenantal confrontation must be to arouse the suspicions and then the ire of the general public. *The protests must expose the immorality of the authorities' cause.* This must be tactical objective number one.

This tactic always requires visible victims, as we shall see in Chapter 4, which deals with covenant sanctions. The visible victims must be those taking the high moral ground. In fact, the public will almost always decide who has taken the high moral ground in terms of the level of victimization. In the case of abortions, the public cares little about what goes on behind the closed doors of the physician's office. They can be lured into caring about what goes on in front of them during the evening television news broadcasts. Their concern will be for the victims of police brutality, not the millions of murdered babies. They cannot feel sentimental about "fetuses" they never see and do not wish to see. They can be made to feel sentimental about the victims of police brutality.

The Christian's primary moral goal must always be witness-bearing: the upholding of God's name through his obedience to God's revealed law. Second, his goal must be to save the greatest number of lives of the judicially innocent. Third, the goal is to change the minds of the voting public. Fourth, the goal must be to bring the murderers to public justice. In short: God first, babies second, votes third, and civil vengeance fourth. We need not be so concerned about civil vengence because God will bring perfect vengeance eternally against evil-doers in eternity.

Life is a positive something. By keeping someone from being unlawfully murdered, a person is performing a positive social act, *just so long as we (or our protest leaders) do not expect the act of protest to lead directly to far more people being murdered.* We must plan our confrontations so that the public, political, and judicial backlash leads to fewer murders, not a public tolerance for more murders. This is inescapably a question of tactics. We must understand the fundamental tactic of non-violent civil disobedience: "The action is the reaction."

Action and Reaction

The model for the minority protester is Gideon's army. Gideon had only a small band of men. He had actually taken two steps to make the group smaller: from 22,000 to 10,000 to 300. God insisted on getting all the credit for the victory (Judges 7:2). With 300 men Gideon faced a huge host of the enemy army, "like grasshoppers for multitude" (Judges 7:12).

He gave each man a trumpet and a pitcher with a lamp in it. Normally, an attacking army would have only a few trumpeters and lamp-carriers. Thus, the defending Midianite army would naturally assume the trumpets and lamps represented a far larger army of Israelites. The band attacked early in the morning, at the time of the changing of the guard (the middle watch). This created confusion in the camp of the enemy. The enemy fled (Judges 7:22).

The action was the reaction. The tactic which Gideon adopted had been designed to put a much larger enemy army to flight. It had rested on the known effects of surprise and misinterpretation of the visible evidence in producing confusion. It made the invaders look more powerful than they were initially. The tactic had rested on the assumption that the reaction of the enemy would destroy them. The action of the attackers was intended to produce a specific set of reactions among the enemy — reactions that would destroy the enemy's ability to resist. Then the small band called the other tribes to help "mop up" the enemy's dispersed and fearful host (Judges 7:23-24). With the victory visible, the other tribes joined the battle. For forty years thereafter, the nation had peace (Judges 8:28).

Gideon's strategy was total victory, but his initial tactic did not involve a direct, full-scale confrontation with a well-organized enemy. Instead, it involved the adoption of a tactic of surprise and deception. The enemy did not expect the Israelites to launch an attack with anything except a full army. When the attack came, they did not know how few they were dealing with. But once the initial victory was achieved, the full army of Israelites assembled to drive out the enemy. The tactic of local confrontation fit the overall strategy of national victory.

Applying This Strategic Principle

Consider the anti-abortion cause. The protesters should be clear in their minds what the overall strategy of the protests should be: the ending of abortion. But this goal will not be achieved through the initial confrontation. Gideon's trumpet was not expected to destroy the enemy at that moment; it was rather a means of gaining a response that would weaken the enemy's potential counter-attack.

It is not the lives of the local unborn babies that the local anti-abortion protest should focus on. There will be few lives saved initially. There is always another abortion mill down the street or outside of town; murderous women always have another opportunity to abort their offspring. What really counts is the total number of lives saved after the voters change their minds or the Supreme Court at last reverses itself on the abortion-on-demand question. Thus, tactics of local civil disobedience must be designed and enforced that produce the sought-after national judicial goal, not the short-term goal of saving lives locally.

What the organized protests should be designed to accomplish is the national reduction of the opportunities to commit legalized murder. This reduction may come because other physicians and hospitals become frightened of the bad publicity, and they then decide to stop making abortions so easy for mothers to buy. The reduction may take place because voters at last change their minds. What must be understood well in advance is this: a protest that temporarily hampers a local clinic but whose tactics turn off the television-viewing or newspaper-reading audience has not been an effective protest. Few lives will be saved locally, and none nationally.

Remember the first rule of civil disobedience: **The action is the reaction**. Before anyone performs acts of civil disobedience, he must have a reasonably clear picture of the reaction he is seeking to produce. He must do all he can to think through the likely responses of his various targets — police, politicians, courts, fellow Christians, and voters — and then take steps to modify his tactics to meet these objectives.

The reaction of the pregnant mothers and their accomplices in crime, the physicians, is predictable, and it should not be weighed very heavily when protest leaders are developing the overall strategy of resistance. Not many of these people will change their minds. Protestors who think otherwise are bound to become frustrated. Frustration can lead to irrational outbursts of violence. This is counter-productive.

The tacticians should assume that there will be an increase in the level of public violence and uncontrolled outrage on the part of the police and other civil authorities. This is what the apostles discovered when they continued preaching. They were publicly flogged, beaten, and left for dead. But this negative reaction must not be provoked by anything except peaceful behavior on the part of protesters. The protest must be designed to make *any* negative reaction against the protesters appear unjust, which it is, because the activity which the authorities are defending is itself unjust. The underlying strategy is to get the politicians to decrease the level of police violence by reversing the unjust law.

The master of this strategy was Mohandas K. Gandhi, a lawyer trained in English common law. Anyone who wants a brief introduction to his strategy of non-violent resistance should rent the videotape of the movie *Gandhi*. View it at least twice, once for the story and once for a closer look at his tactics. While the film is a propaganda piece that was financed in part by the Indian government, it does show how Gandhi deliberately created judicial and political crises that the English civil authorities could not deal with effectively. (For a more critical look at Gandhi's long-ignored life and beliefs, see Richard Grenier, *The Gandhi Nobody Knows* [Thomas Nelson, 1983].)

Escalating Fanaticism

The major danger with the strategy of corporate non-violence

is the possibility of escalating fanaticism on the side of the group
that initiates these non-violent tactics. Mobs do things that those
who make the mob would not do as individuals. There is such a
thing as collective behavior. This is why God holds groups responsible for their actions as well as individuals. This is also why
Christians must know in advance what they are doing and why
they are doing it.

Christians must be confident that it is their absolutely sovereign God who will bring justice in history, and not their own
passions or level of personal commitment. The protest's leaders
must take steps to inform each of the protestors of the covenantal
theology of Christian non-violence. The strategy of Christian non-
violent civil disobedience must honor all five points of the biblical
covenant model if the protest is to be kept within God's lawful
bounds. To keep a legitimate corporate protest from becoming an
undisciplined mob, each individual in the protest group must be
committed to five principles of covenantal confrontation:

1. Confidence in a God who is sovereign;
2. Acceptance of a responsible hierarchical authority governing
   the organized protest;
3. Commitment to self-government under God's law during the
   protest;
4. Faith in a biblical concept of sanctions (blessing and cursing):
   God will bring His judicial sanctions against those who use
   physical violence against the innocent;
5. Faith in the long-term reliability of the promises of God.

Only when these beliefs are part of each participant's thinking will
his instinctive reactions under pressure make him safe to become
a member of an organized non-violent protest.

We can expect escalating fanaticism on the part of the authorities. When everything they do adds to the fire of protest and also
makes them appear as unreasonable people, they get out of control. Gandhi understood this. The more out of control they become, the more martyrs appear on the scene, and the more outra-

geous the civil government appears in the eyes of the public. Thus, one of the key tactics of the protesters is to provoke the fanaticism of the authorities by quiet, prayerful civil behavior. It is the civil government that must be seen by the public as uncivil. ☆

Gandhi mobilized people to march peacefully against the authorities. Wave upon wave of them marched, and were cut down by the clubs of the soldiers or police. This creates a loss of morale in the hearts of the righteous police, and an escalating fury in the hearts of the unrighteous police. Both reactions benefit the long-term goals of the protesters.

The fanaticism of the protester must be the *fanaticism of relentless perseverance.* The protesters simply refuse to go away. Wave upon wave of them come to confront the clubs of the civil government. The theological doctrine that is the foundation of this strategy is called the perseverance of the saints. It is the fifth point of the biblical covenant model: continuity. What is hard on one's cranium is good for one's soul, and also good for the righteous cause.

Counting the Cost

Nevertheless, before getting involved in such a risky and potentially painful protest movement, the prospective protester should first count the cost. So should the organizers.

> For which of you, intending to build a tower, sitteth not down first, and counteth the cost, whether he have sufficient to finish it? Lest haply [it happen], after he hath laid the foundation, and is not able to finish it, all that behold it begin to mock him, This man began to build, and was not able to finish. Or what king, going to make war against another king, sitteth not down first, and consulteth whether he be able with ten thousand to meet him that cometh against him with twenty thousand? Or else, while the other is yet a great way off, he sendeth an ambassage [ambassador or representative], and desireth conditions of peace. So likewise, whosoever he be of you that forsaketh not all that he hath, he cannot be my disciple (Luke 14:28-33).

There should first be an assessment of the enemy's counter-attack. This is very important. We do not have Gideon's access to a prophet who sees in a dream what the ememy's reaction will be (Judges 7:13-14). For example, what if the tactics do close the offices of abortionists? Or what if the government abolishes the physicians' legal right to perform abortions, thereby forcing up the price of the service on the illegal market? What if this new price situation offers a profit opportunity to private industry to sell pills that will abort babies cheaply and easily?

The protester must have a plan of attack in reserve. In October of 1988, the French government forced a semi-private firm to offer an abortion pill for sale after private protests from anti-abortionists had pressured the firm to withdraw the product from the market. Public protests against visible abortionists are not sufficient in a high-technology age. Women will be able to buy such pills in the mail, and a successful protest against physicians could lead to far more abortions if the closing of the centers leads to the marketing of mass-produced abortion pills.

Long-Term Political Mobilization

This means that effective local protests are only the first stage of the protest movement. There must be a willingness on the part of protesters to continue to organize politically, to carry their protest into Congress and the White House. It means that there must be legislation against all chemicals and drugs sold to the public as a means of aborting babies. This will also mean criminal sanctions against manufacturers who sell them and mothers who use them. There must be far more diligence to keep these drugs off the market than efforts to reduce the sale of mind-altering drugs like cocaine, for the use of abortion-inducing drugs cannot be classified under the heading of a "victimless crime."

Today's initial protests are just that: initial. There must be a well thought-out long-term strategy of political mobilization. There must be a counting of the cost. Of course, one important aspect of the visible protests against visible abortion clinics is the recruiting of dedicated people who will stay in the political trenches until chemical abortion agents are outlawed, and the laws have teeth in them. *The action is the reaction.* The reaction of the pro-abortionists should be means of the next action of the anti-abortionists.

This is why the counter-protest argument that "the pro-abortionists will adopt similar tactics" is no argument at all. The political polarization of the nation must escalate if the anti-abortion forces are to receive comprehensive training for the political conquest of the nation. Total political and judicial conquest must be the goal, as surely as it was Gideon's goal: the routing of the enemy throughout the land. Halfway measures will not accomplish this. Halfway measures since 1973 have not accomplished this. We have now reached another stage in the escalation of the conflict. There can be no compromise with evil. There is no "neutral" halfway ground between life and death – not in the abortionist's office, not in the privacy of one's own home, and not in Congress or the U.S. Supreme Court.

The front-cover headline of *U.S. News and World Report* (October 3, 1988) was correct: "Abortion: America's New Civil War." This civil war will escalate as surely as the war against chattel slavery escalated after 1820. It cannot be stopped. It is irrepressible. The magazine posed a front-cover question: "Through the painful confusion, is America ready for the words that heal?" No more than in 1861, when the South wanted national healing only on the basis of these words: "You must permit us to keep our slaves forever without interference!" The North countered with these words of healing: "The nation cannot continue half slave and half free." These were not words of healing; they were words of conflict. The conflict today is equally irrepressible.

This time, however, it is the Christians and not Unitarians who are in charge of the irrepressible protest movement. The Unitarians are all on the other side today. Secular humanists are the "camp of the Midianites." This time, Christians know who their enemies are; they failed to see this in 1820. This time, Christians are initiating the protest, unlike the events after 1820.

We Christians who are protesting abortion today have the moral high ground. We should not worry about the reactions of our enemies. We should design our tactics and our strategy to take advantage of those reactions. We should not lose sight of Gideon's tactical principle (stolen by Saul Alinsky): "The action is the reaction."

But to maintain the moral high ground, we must adhere to the high moral principles we profess. We must understand and honor in all our tactics the biblical moral basis of the protest. We must also understand and honor the biblical *legal* basis of the protest: self-government under God's Bible-revealed law.

Self-Government Under Biblical Law

Self-government under God's law is the biblical legal basis of the organized protest, so visible self-government must also be the foundation of the group's actual tactics. Thus, open displays of anger, shouting, or hysterical crying must be prohibited in advance, and monitored and controlled by the leaders during the actual protest.

The physical presence of a large number of protesters is the primary means of stating the case for justice. The leader or leaders of the particular rally or demonstration must be on hand to speak with the civil authorities and the representatives of the media. The leaders need brief printed summaries of the law of God and how it applies to the particular unjust act that is being challenged. There should also be printed statements on the legality of the protest. Biblical law should be presented first, but also arguments from constitutional law and precedents in common law. Examples of successful non-violent protests in history should also be referred to in the literature. The appeal to higher law is basic; the appeal to precedents is also important. Both heaven and history should be invoked by the spokesmen as justifications of the protest.

It is the printed case for justice that will have the greatest impact on representatives from newspapers and magazines. A forthright, self-confident verbal presentation of the case is effective with all media representatives, but especially television interviewers. Remember: they need 20-second statements to use on the evening news, not long-winded summaries of the history of the world. If the spokesman cannot make the case for justice in three 7-second points or less, postpone the protest.

What must be avoided at all costs is shouting. Shouting is the first stage of a loss of self-control. Silent vigils are basic to successful non-violent protests. The protestors must honor the principle of representation. They must allow the spokesmen to speak in their name.

If any protestor begins to shout, except shouts of pain in response to police violence, the leader must immediately send a delegated representative into the crowd to warn the protestor to be quiet. This makes it clear to the authorities and the press that there is a consistent moral policy governing the protest. Also, it reminds the protester that he or she is under authority.

Shouting is the preliminary sign of escalating emotion. What a man says reflects what he believes. How he says it reflects his state of mind.

> For in many things we offend all. If any man offend not in word, the same is a perfect man, and able also to bridle the whole body. Behold, we put bits in the horses' mouths, that they may obey us; and we turn about their whole body. Behold also the ships, which though they be so great, and are driven of fierce winds, yet are they turned about with a very small helm, whithersoever the governor listeth. Even so the tongue is a little member, and boasteth great things. Behold, how great a matter a little fire kindleth! And the tongue is a fire, a world of iniquity: so is the tongue among our members, that it defileth the whole body, and setteth on fire the course of nature; and it is set on fire of hell (James 3:2-6).

Shouting by protesters is illegitimate in the midst of a non-violent protest. Violence is verbal as well as physical. Let the police do all the shouting. A silent refusal to co-operate is the proper response to police shouting or shouting from opposing protesters.

A far better way to speak out is to sing. Singing drives the authorities nuts. It is also effective on television news clips. The early Christians sang as they were herded into the Roman Colosseum; it impressed many people and outraged others. But it demonstrated that Christians did things differently from other victims of injustice. Singing can be done as loud as you want, although quiet singing is impressive. Song sheets should be handed out to protesters in advance of every local protest. But leaders should recognize that people probably cannot sing enthusiastically hours on end. Singing is appropriate as the police's attacks escalate. It is a way to protest physical injustice under the threat of violence, thereby rechanneling the initial emotional response to scream or fight back physically.

Audible crying by participants must also be avoided. The emotional setting of an abortion clinic is conducive to crying by Christians. As soon as any protester begins crying audibly, except because physical pain inflicted by the police, the leader must send in a representative to ask the crying protester to move away from the group while it is involved in the actual demonstration.

There is also the danger of protesters who carry weapons. Some may do this because they are not committed to non-violent protesting. Others may be *agents provocateurs* who have been sent into the group in order to force a violent demonstration or to embarrass the group publicly. Before anyone is allowed into the main line of protesters, he or she must be asked by a group representative to pull out all pockets or open a purse for inspection. Male representatives can deal with the men, females with women. Every protester must be screened in advance. There must be no exceptions. These are *organized* protests. The organizers must do their work thoroughly. They must make it plain to the public and to the protesters that the group is self-policed.

But Will the Public Respond Favorably?

If the nation is so deeply immersed in sin that the voters do not throw out any politician who allows abortion to continue, how can any Christian legitimately expect the public to change its mind because of a massive organized protest? The answer is: "The same way the voters changed their minds in 1960-64, during the sit-ins in the American South."

What we must understand is that there is still a large Christian electorate. It is unorganized and anything but self-conscious, but it is Christian. It has been buffaloed by the doctrine of judicial supremacy (which was not a doctrine even conceived of by the Constitutional Convention in 1788) and by endless liberal humanist propaganda about "freedom of choice (i.e., murder)" for women.

Even if all the voters were hard-core pagans, the law of God still impresses them. Defending it and enforcing it is a form of evangelism.

> Behold, I have taught you statutes and judgments, even as the LORD my God commanded me, that ye should do so in the land whither ye go to possess it. Keep therefore and do them; for this is your wisdom and your understanding in the sight of the nations, which shall hear all these statutes, and say, Surely this great nation is a wise and understanding people. For what nation is there so great, who hath God so nigh unto them, as the LORD our God is in all things that we call upon him for? And what nation is there so great, that hath statutes and judgments so righteous as all this law, which I set before you this day? (Deut. 4:5-8).

The reason why the defense of God's law works as a means of evangelism and persuasion is because all men have the works of the law written on their hearts — not the law itself, the text says, but at least the work of the law. "For when the Gentiles, which have not the law, do by nature the things contained in the law, these, having not the law, are a law unto themselves: Which shew the work of the law written in their hearts, their conscience also bearing witness, and their thoughts the mean while accusing or else excusing one another" (Romans 2:14-15). Thus, when righteous people conduct their protests righteously, bearing the blows of the civil government (see Chapter 4), the public will eventually respond sympathetically. But the public has to know that the protesters are serious and willing to pay the price. If they are perceived as grandstanders and mere publicity-seekers, the protests will fail in the ultimate objective of getting some evil law changed.

Conclusion

C. S. Lewis, in his novel *That Hideous Strength* (1946), presents in fictional form the nature of the religious warfare of this century. It is subtitled, "A Modern Fairy-Tale for Grown-Ups," but it is in fact a far more accurate literary prophecy than George Orwell's *1984* or Aldous Huxley's *Brave New World*. It describes the coming of a huge government-financed "research foundation" which is fusing experimental science and occultism as a means of taking control of the world. This was also the dream of the Renaissance, as Lewis discusses in Chapter 3 of his brief book, *The Abolition of Man* (1947).

In the novel, one of the characters describes the nature of a long-term escalation of conflict between Christianity and demonic humanism. The character is a college professor of medieval literature, which is what Lewis himself was. Thus, I think this statement represents Lewis' own thinking. It shows why the theological and moral issues are getting clearer as time passes, and why the conflicts between Christians and their opponents will get worse:

> If you dip into any college, or school, or parish, or family — anything you like — at a given point in its history, you always find that there was a time before that point when there was more elbow room and contrasts weren't quite so sharp; and that there's going to be a time after that point when there is even less room for indecision and choices are even more momentous. Good is always getting better and bad is always getting worse: the possibilities of even apparent neutrality are always diminishing. The whole thing is sorting itself out all the time, coming to a point, getting sharper and harder (p. 283).

The ethical issues are getting sharper. The differences between man's law and God's law are becoming clearer. Thus, there has been an escalation of the confrontations between Christians and their opponents. This escalation will continue.

Ultimately, the dividing issues are theological and moral. They cannot be avoided forever. What more and more Christians will begin to see is that there is a war for this world. It is being conducted by the supernatural heads of two kingdoms, God and Satan. The fundamental question in this war is not power, for God could crush Satan in an instant. The fundamental issue is ethical. Whose Word will man believe? Who will man obey? It is the same old issue that Eve faced in the garden. Satan asked: "Hath God said?" Eve knew, but she refused to obey.

In the escalating confrontation between Christianity and humanism today, most Christians know, but like Eve, they simply refuse to obey. And they deeply resent the actions of those Christians who do obey. And as Benjamin Franklin summarized the issue two centuries ago, *resistance to tyrants is obedience to God*.

In summary:

1. Moses' parents and Pharaoh's daughter disobeyed the Pharaoh's law of infanticide.

2. God's law is unchanging in principle because He is unchanging.

3. Changes in the law are made for our sake, not God's.

4. Modern jurisprudence is evolutionary.

5. Modern law is said to change in response to a changing environment.

6. Law has been defined as a prediction regarding what the courts will say.

7. Biblical law is grounded in the Word of God and His perfect justice.

8. The U.S. Supreme Court has often reversed its predecessors' decisions.

9. For a Darwinist, no social law is sacrosanct, for nothing is seen as sacrosanct.

10. Darwinism rejects the idea of a permanent moral order.

11. Christians must oppose unjust civil laws.

12. Darwinists have no moral or legal principle that would allow them to reject this right of Christians (or anyone) to protest.

13. The modern state operates in terms of sentiment and power, not permanent moral principles.

14. Non-violent protests can get out of control.

15. Christians must begin a protest with this presupposition: Protests cannot save mankind.

16. The state cannot save mankind, either.

17. To trust the state to save is to guarantee frustration.

18. Christians must take the moral high ground.

19. The immoral and violent reactions by civil authorities show the public who is on the moral low ground.

20. The political goal of the protest is to arouse the ire of the public against civil injustice.

21. This tactic requires visible victims.

22. The level of victimization identifies those on the high moral ground.

23. The public cares more about visible victims than about the hidden victims (unborn infants).

24. There are four moral goals of the protest: upholding God, saving the greatest number of innocent lives, changing the minds of the public, and bringing evil-doers to justice.

25. Life is a positive goal.

26. The basic tactical principle of protest is Gideon's: **The action is the reaction.**

27. Lives saved nationally should be the national strategic goal, not lives saved locally.

28. The strategy is to change the minds of voters and Supreme Court judges.

29. Protesters should assume that the civil authorities will escalate their violence.

30. Christians must adopt institutional rules that will reduce the likelihood of violence and bad manners within the ranks of the protesters.

31. The protesting group should be committed to the five covenant rules of protest.

32. We need a fanaticism of relentless perseverance.

33. Protesters should first count the cost.

34. The goal is long-term political victory.

35. The protest tactics must be structured in terms of self-government under biblical law.

36. Biblical justice still appeals to the hearts of men (Deuteronomy 4).

37. There will be an escalation of confrontation as time goes on (C. S. Lewis).

38. "Resistance to tyrants is obedience to God." — Ben Franklin

4

WHOSE SANCTIONS WILL PREVAIL?

Then the LORD *said unto me, Proclaim all these words in the cities of Judah, and in the streets of Jerusalem, saying, Hear ye the words of this covenant, and do them. For I earnestly protested unto your fathers in the day that I brought them up out of the land of Egypt, even unto this day, rising early and protesting, saying, Obey my voice. Yet they obeyed not, nor inclined their ear, but walked every one in the imagination of their evil heart: therefore I will bring upon them all the words of this covenant, which I commanded them to do; but they did them not. And the* LORD *said unto me, A conspiracy is found among the men of Judah, and among the inhabitants of Jerusalem. They are turned back to the iniquities of their forefathers, which refused to hear my words; and they went after other gods to serve them: the house of Israel and the house of Judah have broken my covenant which I made with their fathers. Therefore thus saith the* LORD, *Behold, I will bring evil upon them, which they shall not be able to escape; and though they shall cry unto me, I will not hearken unto them (Jeremiah 11:6-11).*

There is no doubt that the prophet Jeremiah functioned as a covenantal agent between God and the innocent people of Judah. The king and his court had become corrupt. Jeremiah proclaimed the terms of the covenant before kings. He was the prosecutor of God's *covenant lawsuit.* But the king chose not to listen. He cut the law of the covenant into pieces and threw the pieces into the fire.

Thus, announced Jeremiah, the nation would fall to the Babylonians.

How would this protect the innocent? Because there would be greater justice under pagan King Nebuchadnezzar than under Jehoiakim. As it turned out, Nebuchadnezzar was converted to true faith in the final year of his life, and God allowed him to write his testimony as a chapter in the Bible – the only formerly pagan writer ever to have this honor (Daniel 4).

Prophetic Confrontation and Political Interposition

While the story is lengthy, it is important for today's Christian to recall the specifics of the historic confrontation between Jeremiah and Baruch his scribe on the one hand, and the king of Judah on the other. It is a grim reminder of the arrogance of rulers in the face of a looming national crisis. I include it in full detail because Christian critics of public protests by Christians insist that the protesters show that their arguments are based on the Bible. Unfortunately, Christians frequently prefer not to read the Bible, but instead rely on someone's summary of the Bible. Reading the Bible takes too much time, they think. They prefer to skip over the biblical text and "get to the heart of the matter," as if the biblical text were not the heart of the matter.

The incident began with a fast which the people themselves called. They perceived that a national crisis was imminent. In this respect, the spiritual decline of the people had not yet reached rock bottom. They still recognized, however dimly, that *there is a cause-and-effect relationship in history between covenantal rebellion and national catastrophe*. The Babylonians were almost literally at the gates of the city, and the people wanted to do something to avoid the nation's looming defeat. They allowed Baruch, Jeremiah's scribe, to read the words that God had declared to Jeremiah:

> And it came to pass in the fifth year of Jehoiakim the son of Josiah king of Judah, in the ninth month, that they proclaimed a fast before the LORD to all the people in Jerusalem, and to all the people that came from the cities of Judah unto Jerusalem. Then

read Baruch in the book the words of Jeremiah in the house of the
LORD, in the chamber of Gemariah the son of Shaphan the scribe,
in the higher court, at the entry of the new gate of the LORD'S
house, in the ears of all the people (Jeremiah 36:9-10).

An agent of the lower magistrates was in the crowd, and he
then took the message to his associates.

> When Michaiah the son of Gemariah, the son of Shaphan, had
> heard out of the book all the words of the LORD, Then he went
> down into the king's house, into the scribe's chamber: and, lo, all
> the princes sat there, even Elishama the scribe, and Delaiah the
> son of Shemaiah, and Elnathan the son of Achbor, and Gemariah
> the son of Shaphan, and Zedekiah the son of Hananiah, and all the
> princes. Then Michaiah declared unto them all the words that he
> had heard, when Baruch read the book in the ears of the people.
> Therefore all the princes sent Jehudi the son of Nethaniah, the son
> of Shelemiah, the son of Cushi, unto Baruch, saying, Take in thine
> hand the roll wherein thou hast read in the ears of the people, and
> come. So Baruch the son of Neriah took the roll in his hand, and
> came unto them. And they said unto him, Sit down now, and read
> it in our ears. So Baruch read it in their ears (Jeremiah 36:11-16).

The lower magistrates decided at that point to listen to the
words of the prophet. The people had initiated the national fast;
now the rulers felt led by the example set by the people. When
they heard the message, they decided that the prophet's warning
should be taken seriously. Then they made a fundamental decision. They decided to serve as judicial intermediaries between
Baruch and the king. They took a legal stand: *interposition.*

> Now it came to pass, when they had heard all the words, they
> were afraid both one and other, and said unto Baruch, We will
> surely tell the king of all these words. And they asked Baruch,
> saying, Tell us now, How didst thou write all these words at his
> mouth? Then Baruch answered them, He pronounced all these
> words unto me with his mouth, and I wrote them with ink in the
> book. Then said the princes unto Baruch, Go, hide thee, thou and
> Jeremiah; and let no man know where ye be. And they went in to
> the king into the court, but they laid up the roll in the chamber of

Elishama the scribe, and told all the words in the ears of the king.
So the king sent Jehudi to fetch the roll: and he took it out of
Elishama the scribe's chamber. And Jehudi read it in the ears of
the king, and in the ears of all the princes which stood beside the
king (36:14-21).

The king by now had heard that the people had called a fast
and had listened to Baruch. Now he was being confronted by his
subordinate officials. They were telling him that they had listened
and that he should, too. Thus, the covenantal message had moved
to the pinnacle of civil government. What would the king do? How
would he respond?

A Representative Act of National Rebellion

The king had to respond covenantally. He could act as a
covenant-keeper or as a covenant-breaker. He could "cut the
covenant" through an act of covenant renewal. This would require
him to make public repentance as the representative of the nation.
He understood this, and he decided to cut the covenant literally
rather than ethically.

> Now the king sat in the winterhouse in the ninth month: and
> there was a fire on the hearth burning before him. And it came to
> pass, that when Jehudi had read three or four leaves, he cut it with
> the penknife, and cast it into the fire that was on the hearth, until
> all the roll was consumed in the fire that was on the hearth
> (Jeremiah 36:22-23).

At this point, the lower magistrates could have intervened and
demanded that the king renew the covenant through representative repentance. This would have been a revolution. It would have
been based on the doctrine of interposition: lower magistrates
overturning a superior's decision to defy God in his capacity as a
public official. But the lower magistrates decided to stand with the
king. His courage gave them courage.

> Yet they were not afraid, nor rent their garments, neither the
> king, nor any of his servants that heard all these words. Neverthe-
> less Elnathan and Delaiah and Gemariah had made intercession

to the king that he would not burn the roll: but he would not hear them. But the king commanded Jerahmeel the son of Hammelech, and Seraiah the son of Azriel, and Shelemiah the son of Abdeel, to take Baruch the scribe and Jeremiah the prophet: but the LORD hid them (Jeremiah 36:24-26).

Jeremiah and Baruch could have stayed hidden. After all, they had confronted people, magistrates, and king, without success. They could in good conscience wait for the Lord to bring His sanctions. But Jeremiah understood the biblical principle of the double witness. Jeremiah decided to bring God's covenant lawsuit against the king a second time.

> Then the word of the LORD came to Jeremiah, after that the king had burned the roll, and the words which Baruch wrote at the mouth of Jeremiah, saying, Take thee again another roll, and write in it all the former words that were in the first roll, which Jehoiakim the king of Judah hath burned. And thou shalt say to Jehoiakim king of Judah, Thus saith the LORD; Thou hast burned this roll, saying, Why hast thou written therein, saying, The king of Babylon shall certainly come and destroy this land, and shall cause to cease from thence man and beast? Therefore thus saith the LORD of Jehoiakim king of Judah; He shall have none to sit upon the throne of David: and his dead body shall be cast out in the day to the heat, and in the night to the frost. And I will punish him and his seed and his servants for their iniquity; and I will bring upon them, and upon the inhabitants of Jerusalem, and upon the men of Judah, all the evil that I have pronounced against them; but they hearkened not (Jeremiah 36:27-31).

But they hearkened not. And in hearkening not, they sealed their doom. Babylon invaded, and Judah fell. The people, the magistrates, the king, and even Jeremiah went into exile in Egypt.

Speaking Prophetically Today

It is frequently said by Christians who are upset by the sight of other Christians who carry picket signs or in other ways publicly protest against public evil, "Who do you think you are? You're not prophets. You have no right to act like prophets." This accusation is true, if by "prophet" we mean people who are uniquely called by God to confront kings. There are no more prophets any more. For that matter, there are no more kings. But Christians can speak prophetically — analogous to the way that prophets spoke.

Did Jeremiah try to organize a public protest? No, he did not have to. He was content to see Judah fall to the Babylonians. It was his task to warn the rulers of God's impending wrath, but he did not organize politically to force them out of office. That would not have been possible. Jeremiah organized no protests because he knew that God had given over the nation to its enemies. God was fed up:

> Therefore thou shalt speak unto them this word; Thus saith the LORD God of Israel, Every bottle shall be filled with wine: and they shall say unto thee, Do we not certainly know that every bottle shall be filled with wine? Then shalt thou say unto them, Thus saith the LORD, Behold, I will fill all the inhabitants of this land, even the kings that sit upon David's throne, and the priests, and the prophets, and all the inhabitants of Jerusalem, with drunkenness. And I will dash them one against another, even the fathers and the sons together, saith the LORD: I will not pity, nor spare, nor have mercy, but destroy them (Jeremiah 13:12-14).

In fact, it is because we are not prophetically endowed regarding the specific future that we Christians *must* speak out. We must preach God's Word faithfully. We are required by God to speak *prophetically*: bringing to the attention of all men the judicial terms of God's covenant, personal and corporate, warning them of the covenant's promised negative sanctions — sanctions that are applied in history by God to His enemies, personally and corporately.

There are those who say that God no longer applies his sanctions in history. These are false prophets. In Jeremiah's day, God promised to deal with them harshly. He also promised to deal harshly with those who listen to them and believe them. Men should take heed:

> Then said I, Ah, Lord GOD! behold, the prophets say unto

them, Ye shall not see the sword, neither shall ye have famine; but I will give you assured peace in this place. Then the LORD said unto me, The prophets prophesy lies in my name: I sent them not, neither have I commanded them, neither spake unto them: they prophesy unto you a false vision and divination, and a thing of nought, and the deceit of their heart. Therefore thus saith the LORD concerning the prophets that prophesy in my name, and I sent them not, yet they say, Sword and famine shall not be in this land; By sword and famine shall those prophets be consumed. And the people to whom they prophesy shall be cast out in the streets of Jerusalem because of the famine and the sword; and they shall have none to bury them, them, their wives, nor their sons, nor their daughters: for I will pour their wickedness upon them (Jeremiah 14:13-16).

Stages of Avoiding God's Negative Physical Sanctions

Once sin is indulged in, there will be negative sanctions imposed by God on the sinner or a substitute. Negative sanctions are inevitable. The only way to escape them is for someone to intervene and bear them in place of the sinner. What if the sinner persists in his sin? What if he rejects the free offer of personal interposition that Jesus Christ the sin-bearer has made? Then God threatens to escalate the level of sanctions.

Those under the authority of wicked rulers are inevitably involved in their corporate sins. This is because all authority is hierarchical. The wicked rulers represent the whole society, even including good men. This is analogous to a military chain of command. As surely as competent military troops are defeated if the commander makes bad decisions, so can righteous people be placed under the general sanctions God brings against unrighteous rulers.

This is why churches are required by God to call wickedness to account, which includes warning all men, including rulers, of God's covenantal sanctions. The only way for righteous men to avoid these sanctions is for them to become true watchmen on the tower. The churches of a nation must confront the specific evil that threatens to bring down God's wrath if the sin is not stopped. They must preach against the specific sin, organize people to fight against it, and teach them how to petition governments and organize politically.

If political mobilization is impossible (as in Communist nations) or fails to produce results (as has been the case in the United States since *Roe v. Wade* was handed down in 1973), then the churches must advance to the next stage. This involves calling down God's wrath on the offending civil governors or judges. The best models here are the so-called imprecatory psalms. They are not prayed in public very often in modern churches. They are forgotten, or worse, they have become an embarrassment. But their use as part of formal worship is clearly called for, or else God would not have put them in the psalms, which are intended to be sung in public. A good example of an imprecatory psalm is Psalm 83.

> Keep not thou silence, O God: hold not thy peace, and be not *Obama* still, O God. For, lo, thine enemies make a tumult: and they that *Hillary* hate thee have lifted up the head. They have taken crafty counsel against thy people, and consulted against thy hidden ones (Psalm 83:1-3).

> Do unto them as unto the Midianites; as to Sisera, as to Jabin, at the brook of Kison: Which perished at En-dor: they became as dung for the earth. Make their nobles like Oreb, and like Zeeb: yea, all their princes as Zebah, and as Zalmunna: Who said, Let us take to ourselves the houses of God in possession. O my God, make them like a wheel; as the stubble before the wind. As the fire burneth a wood, and as the flame setteth the mountains on fire; So persecute them with thy tempest, and make them afraid with thy storm. Fill their faces with shame; that they may seek thy name, O LORD. Let them be confounded and troubled for ever; yea, let them be put to shame, and perish: That men may know that thou, whose name alone is JEHOVAH, art the most high over all the earth (Psalm 83:9-18).

Churches that are too embarrassed to pray such prayers against those who murder judicially innocent unborn infants do not understand the looming problem facing modern society. The sanctions are coming. (If AIDS is any indication, as I believe that it is, the sanction is already here.) If praying an imprecatory psalm is a worse offense in the eyes of a Christian than the crime of abortion, then that Christian is fleeing from God, one way or another.

The task of being an intercessor in prayer is not denied by Christians. A man intercedes at the throne of God in the name of others. This is the biblical meaning of the word *saint*. It is someone who has lawful access to God's *sanctuary*. He is *set apart* because he is morally *sanctified* by God's imputation of Christ's righteousness to him. But a saint brings *sanctions*. He calls for God to impose physical sanctions on His enemies. And God may then call him to move from being an intercessor to an interposer. He calls him to interpose *positive sanctions* — the preservation of a judicially innocent life — by bringing upon himself the negative sanction of the state.

The next stage of protest is civil disobedience. Christians jam the doorways of the abortion mills. While the timing of each stage of escalating prophetic protest is difficult to judge, there is no doubt that doing nothing is in fact doing something. It is allowing society to come under the sanctions of God in history. It is interesting that the following passage is used by trainers in evangelism (soul-winning) in the personal salvation sense, but not in its corporate covenantal transgression and judgment sense, which is what the passage deals with:

> Son of man, speak to the children of thy people, and say unto them, When I bring the sword upon a land, if the people of the land take a man of their coasts, and set him for their watchman: If when he seeth the sword come upon the land, he blow the trumpet, and warn the people; Then whosoever heareth the sound of the trumpet, and taketh not warning; if the sword come, and take him away, his blood shall be upon his own head. He heard the sound of the trumpet, and took not warning; his blood shall be upon him. But he that taketh warning shall deliver his soul. But if the watchman see the sword come, and blow not the trumpet,

and the people be not warned; if the sword come, and take any person from among them, he is taken away in his iniquity; but his blood will I require at the watchman's hand. So thou, O son of man, I have set thee a watchman unto the house of Israel; therefore thou shalt hear the word at my mouth, and warn them from me. When I say unto the wicked, O wicked man, thou shalt surely die; if thou dost not speak to warn the wicked from his way, that wicked man shall die in his iniquity; but his blood will I require at thine hand. Nevertheless, if thou warn the wicked of his way to turn from it; if he do not turn from his way, he shall die in his iniquity; but thou hast delivered thy soul (Ezekiel 33:2-9).

See what it says? If the watchman refuses to warn the people of their ethical transgression, *then the negative sanctions will be applied to the watchman.* This is not figurative language. This is not to be allegorized away. This is God speaking, and His Word is sure.

This is the language of the sword. The text shows us that it is not the prophet who wields the sword; the prophet wields the covenant. God does not call the prophet or watchman to execute physical judgment on sinners; he calls on him to warn sinners of impending physical judgment. God uses other agents than prophets to wield His sword or rod of wrath. But He does bring it eventually.

If the church remains silent in our day, then we can expect the sword, the famine, and the plague. Most Christians deny this fact, either openly or in their hearts. If so, they have become false prophets, if only to themselves: "Then said I, Ah, Lord GOD! behold, the prophets say unto them, Ye shall not see the sword, neither shall ye have famine; but I will give you assured peace in this place" (Jeremiah 14:13).

There is one final stage of protest: armed revolution. This is lawfully launched only by lower magistrates. This is the Protestant doctrine called the doctrine of interposition. John Calvin discussed it in Chapter 20 of Book 4 of his *Institutes of the Christian Religion.* It was also taught by the anonymous "Junius Brutus" in the *Vindiciae Contra Tyrannos,* which was published in 1581, also known as *A Defence of Liberty Against Tyrants.* This book was translated into

English in 1689, the year following the Glorious Revolution of Parliament against King James II. Many of the arguments for lawful revolution found in John Locke's *Second Treatise of Government* (1690) were taken from the *Vindiciae*. The book was known to leaders of the American Revolution nine decades later.

If the doctrine of interposition is false, then the American Revolution has no grounding in the Bible, no moral or legal justification in the eyes of God. Thus, those Christians who say confidently that all revolutionary violence is wrong have become the spiritual heirs of the Tories — not just those who opposed the American Revolution, but those who opposed the revolution of 1689. While such views have existed in history, they were opposed by the Whig tradition of lawful revolution against tyranny. Ben Franklin, freethinker though he was, recognized the Christian roots of this doctrine, and so proposed that the Great Seal of the United States be a picture of the Israelites crossing the Red Sea, with this motto: "Resistance to Tyrants is Obedience to God."

If lower magistrates refuse to take up arms against a corrupt central government, or if they are defeated in the attempt, then God will use outside agents to bring judgment. The point is, the doctrine of interposition is not strictly political or military; it is covenantal. God will raise up those who will act as His agents in bringing injustice to a halt. Someone will intervene in the name of the victimized innocents.

Warning: at each stage, the sanctions get worse.

In Defense of "Single-Issue" Politics

Both God and Satan run their kingdoms in terms of the five-point covenant model. The authorized agents of both supernatural beings threaten to impose sanctions. Thus, when the watchman-prophet begins to challenge the existing social evils of the day, he can expect retaliation.

This happened to Jeremiah. The lower civil magistrates intervened themselves into the affairs of the king. They persuaded him to allow them to put Jeremiah in a dungeon. We learn from this that there is evil intervention in life.

Then Zedekiah the king commanded that they should commit Jeremiah into the court of the prison, and that they should give him daily a piece of bread out of the bakers' street, until all the bread in the city were spent. Thus Jeremiah remained in the court of the prison. Then Shephatiah the son of Mattan, and Gedaliah the son of Pashur, and Jucal the son of Shelemiah, and Pashur the son of Malchiah, heard the words that Jeremiah had spoken unto all the people, saying, Thus saith the LORD, He that remaineth in this city shall die by the sword, by the famine, and by the pestilence: but he that goeth forth to the Chaldeans shall live; for he shall have his life for a prey, and shall live. Thus saith the LORD, This city shall surely be given into the hand of the king of Babylon's army, which shall take it. Therefore the princes said unto the king, We beseech thee, let this man be put to death: for thus he weakeneth the hands of the men of war that remain in this city, and the hands of all the people, in speaking such words unto them: for this man seeketh not the welfare of this people, but the hurt. Then Zedekiah the king said, Behold, he is in your hand: for the king is not he that can do any thing against you. Then took they Jeremiah, and cast him into the dungeon of Malchiah the son of Hammelech, that was in the court of the prison: and they let down Jeremiah with cords. And in the dungeon there was no water, but mire: so Jeremiah sunk in the mire (Jeremiah 37:21-38:6).

This act of evil-minded intervention against the protesting prophet was countered by a righteous man who then intervened to help the prophet. The king was double-minded and confused, and in such situations, there will be a war for the mind and support of the king. Today, the national civil government of the United States is equally double-minded and confused, which makes intervention a way of life for protesters, both good and evil. This is why there has been a growth of "single-issue" politics and single-issue pressure groups. This is a wholesome political development, one which those on the high moral ground should expect to benefit from. As Christian political lobbyist Larry Pratt says, "Whose direct-mail piece is likely to gain the most response, the one that protests the killing of babies or the one that upholds 'the woman's right to choose'?" Single-issue politics would not have the politically disruptive effects that are criticized by the would-be "peace-keepers" of the land if the voting public and their political representatives were not double-minded morally, if they were not so unwilling to obey God's law. We need more "single-issue protesters" like Ebed-melech:

> Now when Ebed-melech the Ethiopian, one of the eunuchs which was in the king's house, heard that they had put Jeremiah in the dungeon; the king then sitting in the gate of Benjamin; Ebed-melech went forth out of the king's house, and spake to the king, saying, My lord the king, these men have done evil in all that they have done to Jeremiah the prophet, whom they have cast into the dungeon; and he is like to die for hunger in the place where he is: for there is no more bread in the city. Then the king commanded Ebed-melech the Ethiopian, saying, Take from hence thirty men with thee, and take up Jeremiah the prophet out of the dungeon, before he die. So Ebed-melech took the men with him, and went into the house of the king under the treasury, and took thence old cast clouts and old rotten rags, and let them down by cords into the dungeon to Jeremiah. And Ebed-melech the Ethiopian said unto Jeremiah, Put now these old cast clouts and rotten rags under thine armholes under the cords. And Jeremiah did so. So they drew up Jeremiah with cords, and took him up out of the dungeon: and Jeremiah remained in the court of the prison. (Jeremiah 38:7-13).

Jeremiah was placed under physical sanctions. An intercessor intervened on his behalf and gained his release. Ebed-melech was a righteous man, for he risked the king's wrath by intervening in this fashion. Queen Esther did the same thing for her people, the Jews, who were about to be placed under the king's deadly sanctions because of Haman's evil intercession against them.

Counter-Attack: Physical Sanctions

There should be little doubt in the minds of those who take up the covenant task of challenging rulers in God's name that the civil rulers will strike back, perhaps literally. If civil rulers will tolerate and even authorize (i.e., *sanction*) the profit-seeking murder of the innocent, then they will surely tolerate the persecution of those who interpose themselves in between the murderers and their judicially innocent victims. The rulers recognize clearly that these watchmen are calling rulers to judicial account before God and men when they interpose themselves between the murderous sanctions of the abortionists and their intended victims. The more public and physical the interposition, the more resentful and revengeful the morally corrupt and judicially blinded rulers will be. They will escalate their negative sanctions as surely as God will escalate His.

The physical interposition of the saints is biblically legitimate because the sanctions of the murderers are illegitimately physical. Because the interposition of the saints is physical, the sanctions applied by the public authorities are also likely to be physical. From the very beginning of the protest, the question is not "sanctions vs. no sanctions." The question is: Whose sanctions? When the confrontation escalates, the question is not physical sanctions vs. no physical sanctions. The question is: Whose physical sanctions? Which physical sanctions?

What all Christian protesters must understand before they get involved in acts of physical interposition is this: without the support of the lower magistrates, they cannot lawfully and covenantally impose negative physical sanctions against the civil authorities. *Non-violent physical interposition is a positive physical sanction for the unborn child and therefore a negative physical sanction against attempted murderers, but it is not a negative physical sanction against the civil magistrate.* There is nothing in principle that says that protesters cannot lawfully and covenantally impose the physical sanction of bodily interposition in between criminals and victims.

If the interposer predicts that making a citizen's arrest of the murderers will not be sustained in court, then he may choose to test the law in other ways. The way he does this biblically is to become the *covenantal stripe-bearer*. He interposes himself physically in between the criminal and the intended victim, and thereby risks taking the physical punishment that the murderer's agents, the police, may impose on all protesters. Jesus Christ provides us with the biblical model of passive stripe-bearing.

> He is despised and rejected of men; a man of sorrows, and acquainted with grief: and we hid as it were our faces from him; he was despised, and we esteemed him not. Surely he hath borne our griefs, and carried our sorrows: yet we did esteem him stricken, smitten of God, and afflicted. But he was wounded for our transgressions, he was bruised for our iniquities: the chastisement of our peace was upon him; and with his stripes we are healed. All we like sheep have gone astray; we have turned every one to his own way; and the LORD hath laid on him the iniquity of us all. He was oppressed, and he was afflicted, yet he opened not his mouth: he is brought as a lamb to the slaughter, and as a sheep before her shearers is dumb, so he openeth not his mouth. He was taken from prison and from judgment: and who shall declare his generation? for he was cut off out of the land of the living: for the transgression of my people was he stricken. And he made his grave with the wicked, and with the rich in his death; because he had done no violence, neither was any deceit in his mouth. Yet it pleased the LORD to bruise him; he hath put him to grief: when thou shalt make his soul an offering for sin, he shall see his seed, he shall prolong his days, and the pleasure of the LORD shall prosper in his hand. He shall see of the travail of his soul, and shall be satisfied: by his knowledge shall my righteous servant justify many; for he shall bear their iniquities. Therefore will I divide him a portion with the great, and he shall divide the spoil with the strong; because he hath poured out his soul unto death: and he was numbered with the transgressors; and he bare the sin of many, and made intercession for the transgressors (Isaiah 53:3-12).

The Christian cannot bear another man's sin, but he can serve as Jesus Christ did as an interposer. He can pay part of the historical price owed by the sinner. If by taking the beating administered by an officer of corrupt rulers, he can thereby turn public opinion and save the lives of the innocent, he can delay or eliminate the judgment of God on the whole society.

Being an interposer in the face of physical danger is another aspect of being an intercessor. As a stripe-bearer, the interposer places himself as God's agent of positive sanctions. God's positive sanctions (blessings) will come to the whole society if the voters see what their civil representatives are doing, and then replace them.

Should Christians Resist Public Evil?

Chapter 2 begins with the seemingly contradictory biblical passages regarding obedience to civil magistrates. If we understand the covenant, we understand how these two principles fit together: the doctrine of hierarchical authority. The state is under God. The Christian who protests a biblically evil law is being faithful to God. He is calling the rulers to repentance by a public stand against a bad law. The Christian must obey the terms of God's covenant.

A similar and even parallel seeming dilemma is found in these two passages:

> But I say unto you, That ye resist not evil: but whosoever shall smite thee on thy right cheek, turn to him the other also (Matthew 5:39).

> Submit yourselves therefore to God. Resist the devil, and he will flee from you (James 4:7).

The Christian is not called to strike the king's agent on his cheek; rather, he is to accept the blows on his own cheek. The context of this passage is bondage. Israel was under the political rule of the Roman Empire. Jesus was instructing His followers not to become violent political revolutionaries. Submit to stronger political and military power for the time being, He said. But this did not mean that they should not oppose civil rulers who were evil. It meant that the resistance program should be non-violent. He was calling His followers to non-violent protests: to take the blows of the unrighteous rulers.

James was saying the same thing. Christians are to submit to

God but resist the temptations of the devil. The devil cannot tolerate moral resistance. He will eventually flee from those who display the moral will to resist. This does not deny Jesus' principle of turning the other cheek. Non-violent resistance is a way to resist the devil, but a peaceful form. It is an appropriate form of resistance for those who are under the judicial bondage of morally corrupt rulers.

The point that Jesus was making is that the protester must be willing to endure the physical sanctions imposed by the enemy. This is always the risk of becoming a non-violent protester of public unrighteousness. The protest is covenantally legitimate, but only if the protesters bear the physical sanctions of the police, and the economic sanctions imposed by the courts.

In order to reverse the prior ruling of a higher court, protesters should demand a jury trial. Every protester should demand this. If they cannot afford to do this financially, then other resisters should dig into their wallets and finance these people's legal defense. The goal is to get at least one test case that reverses the existing legal precedent. If every protester simply forfeits bond and refuses to be tried, they do not get a test case.

Conclusion

The prophet's role is to bring a covenant lawsuit against the society. He brings it especially to the civil magistrates. They act representatively in the name of the people. The survival of the nation is at stake; the ruler can make or break the nation depending on his response to the prophet.

The people are given an opportunity to hear the terms of the lawsuit. So are the lesser magistrates. They are sovereign, not the king. They can interpose themselves judicially and force the king to renew the covenant with God. On a few occasions in Israel's history, they did. When King Saul issued his foolish rule that nobody could eat during the battle with the Philistines, and

Jonathan, just before his victory, ate honey. the king was ready to execute him.

> Then Saul said to Jonathan, Tell me what thou hast done. And Jonathan told him, and said, I did but taste a little honey with the end of the rod that was in mine hand, and, lo, I must die. And Saul answered, God do so and more also: for thou shalt surely die, Jonathan. And the people said unto Saul, Shall Jonathan die, who hath wrought this great salvation in Israel? God forbid: as the LORD liveth, there shall not one hair of his head fall to the ground; for he hath wrought with God this day. So the people rescued Jonathan, that he died not" (I Samuel 14:43-45).

But such occurrences were rare in Israel's history. Nothing like this took place in Jeremiah's day. And so Judah fell.

The goal of the prophet is to bring God's covenant lawsuit against the nation. He is to bring it publicly. He must capture the attention of the whole nation and its civil and ecclesiastical leaders. This means that the confrontation must be public. The confrontation is ultimately covenantal, but it must also be verbal and visible confrontation.

This is why in today's world the media is vital. It is through public confrontation between God's prophets and the nation that the issue is made visible. Gandhi knew, Martin Luther King knew, and the radicals of the late 1960's knew: the media is the way to the people.

It is time for Christians to bring covenant lawsuit. If they do not, or if they do it ineffectively, God will bring His sanctions. At that point, a Christian does not want to be a watchman on the watchtower who had failed to sound the warning. The warning above all is covenantal.

In summary:

1. Jeremiah was a covenantal agent of God.
2. He brought God's covenant lawsuit before Judah.
3. The people initially listened to Jeremiah's message (given through Baruch the scribe).
4. The lesser magistrates initially listened.

5. The king cut the scroll into pieces and tossed them in the fire.

6. The lesser magistrates sided with the king.

7. Jeremiah sent another scroll: the double witness.

8. Christians can lawfully speak prophetically today.

9. Christians must protest publicly because we do not know whether God has given up the nation to the invaders.

10. There are always false prophets who deny God's covenant sanctions in history, especially negative sanctions.

11. Churches should call publicly to account wicked behavior by civil rulers.

12. Churches should use the imprecatory psalms – psalms of negative judgment.

13. The intercessor is a saint.

14. The saint has access to God's holy sanctuary.

15. The saint is God's counsellor.

16. The saint calls down God's sanctions.

17. The next stage of protest is civil disobedience.

18. The watchman who fails to warn men of the impending negative sanctions must bear those sanctions personally.

19. The final stage of protest is armed revolution: corporate interposition.

20. This can be organized lawfully only by lower magistrates.

21. "Single-issue" political action is biblical.

22. When the enemy imposes negative sanctions, the proper response is personal interposition, either legal or physical.

23. Non-violent interposition does not require the approval of lesser magistrates.

24. Jesus was the ultimate interposer.

25. He bore the sanctions of God, administered by unjust men.

26. The interposer may sometimes bear the state's physical sanctions.

27. Christians must resist the evil one.

28. This resistance can be non-violent.

29. If protesters are unwilling to bear the state's sanctions voluntarily, then they should not escalate the level of protest.

30. The confrontation is ultimately covenantal: bringing God's covenant lawsuit.

5

COVENANT-BREAKING AND
SOCIAL DISCONTINUITY

Thou shalt not make unto thee any graven image, or any likeness of any thing that is in heaven above, or that is in the earth beneath, or that is in the water under the earth: Thou shalt not bow down thyself to them, nor serve them: for I the LORD thy God am a jealous God, visiting the iniquity of the fathers upon the children unto the third and fourth generation of them that hate me; And shewing mercy unto thousands of them that love me, and keep my commandments (Exodus 20:4-6).

The accusation is frequently made against those Christians who get involved in public protests, especially non-violent interposition, that they are revolutionaries. "The Bible is opposed to revolution," the protesters are told by fellow Christians. "Your tactics are immoral; they could lead to revolution!"

The Bible tells a very different story. The Bible teaches that *social continuity is based exclusively on covenant-keeping.* Social continuity is a gift from God to obedient societies. In contrast, a revolutionary break in society is God's judgment on corporate covenant-breaking: the negative sanction of *disinheritance.* It is ethical rebellion that brings the radical discontinuity of revolution. It is the voting public's silence or passive acquiescence to judicially sanctioned acts of covenant-breaking that bring the painful social discontinuities of history: war, famine, plague, and political revolution.

103

How Many Generations of Peace?

The third commandment says, "I the LORD thy God am a jealous God, visiting the iniquity of the fathers upon the children unto the third and fourth generation of them that hate me; And shewing mercy unto thousands of them that love me, and keep my commandments."

When God says that He visits the iniquity of the fathers, He means that He visits rebellious society and sees it, generation after generation. God does not break into history with His comprehensive covenant sanctions at the first sign of national iniquity. He is patient. He is merciful. He extends time to that society for public repentance. But He visits iniquity, generation after generation. He sees and does not forget. Then, in the third or fourth generation after the initial public iniquity began, He brings His negative covenantal sanctions. This is the essence of social discontinuity. This is the essence of revolution. It is God's revolution against covenantal unrighteousness.

In contrast, God shows mercy unto thousands of those who love Him and keep His commandments. What does "thousands" refer to? It has to mean *thousands of generations*. The words "third and fourth generation" are contrasted to "thousands."

Does this mean that history will go on for at least 40,000 years (i.e., 40 years per generation)? Not necessarily. The term "thousands" is symbolic. It means "till the end of time." God's covenant blessings are continuous and endless if men remain faithful to the terms of God's covenant. Generation after generation, people inherit the blessings of God. This is the covenantal doctrine of inheritance. It is the basis of anti-revolutionary social continuity.

The curses come at the end of much shorter intervals. While good is allowed to compound and grow over time, evil is cut short in the midst of time. Social continuity is available only to those societies that remain covenantally faithful to God. This is the positive sanction of God: blessing. Social discontinuity is the inevitable result of corporate covenantal rebellion that persists for three or four generations. This is the negative sanction of God: cursing.

The Perseverance of the Saints

A saint, if you remember, means someone who has access to God's holy (set apart) *sanctuary*. Through prayer, formal worship, and the sacrament of communion (the Lord's Supper), the individual Christian gains entrance into the very throne room of God. He becomes a *counsellor to God*, just as Moses was a counsellor. Through prayer, the saint counsels God. He offers suggestions. Moses' example is representative of what it is we are to do. Moses the counsellor challenged God not to do what He said He would do, namely, destroy the Israelites in the wilderness.

> And Moses besought the LORD his God, and said, LORD, why doth thy wrath wax hot against thy people, which thou hast brought forth out of the land of Egypt with great power, and with a mighty hand? Wherefore should the Egyptians speak, and say, For mischief did he bring them out, to slay them in the mountains, and to consume them from the face of the earth? Turn from thy fierce wrath, and repent of this evil against thy people. Remember Abraham, Isaac, and Israel, thy servants, to whom thou swarest by thine own self, and saidst unto them, I will multiply your seed as the stars of heaven, and all this land that I have spoken of will I give unto your seed, and they shall inherit it for ever (Exodus 32:11-13).

The significant fact here is that God listened to Moses' counsel and heeded it. "And the LORD repented of the evil which he thought to do unto his people" (Exodus 32:14).

What was the basis of Moses' appeal? God's honor. He appealed to God's past promises to Abraham, Isaac, and Israel (Jacob). These promises had been based on God's *covenant* with them. He had promised an *inheritance* to Israel. Would God cut off this inheritance in the midst of history? If so, then the nations round about would call God a liar, a deity impotent to bring His Word to pass in history. He did not appeal to God in terms of the good intentions or righteousness of the Israelites; he appealed to the good intent and righteousness of God. He appealed to God's name. God listened to this prayer, and answered it as Moses suggested.

This is what it means to pray. You become God's *counsellor*. As a saint, you are *set apart*. You are granted access to God, who brings His will to bear *in history*. His holy (set apart) will is seen in His *sanctions*: blessing and cursing. They are seen long term. The evidence of His positive sanctions is *continuity*, meaning corporate inheritance, generation after generation. The evidence of His negative sanctions is *discontinuity*, meaning corporate disinheritance.

The True Saint Perseveres

Moses persevered with the people of God for four decades. God also persevered with them through Moses, His representative covenantal agent. It was the sign of God's covenantal faithfulness to Moses and Moses' covenantal faithfulness to God that Moses was a leader throughout this period.

Moses committed one major sin. He tapped the rock with his rod in order to get it to bring forth water for the people. This was in defiance of God's instruction that he simply speak to the rock (Num. 20:7-12). Moses was to some extent still under the influence of Egyptian magic. The occult magician believes in *power through physical manipulation*. Magic teaches, "as above, so below." If you can manipulate the local environment, you can control the cosmic environment. (If you wonder why modern humanism's hypothesis of environmental determinism is a first cousin to "primitive" magic, search no farther. Environmental determinism teaches that you can remake mankind ethically by remaking man's environment economically through politics.)

What is significant is the nature of God's punishment on Moses: *personal disinheritance*. "And the LORD spake unto Moses and Aaron, Because ye believed me not, to sanctify me in the eyes of the children of Israel, therefore ye shall not bring this congregation into the land which I have given them" (Numbers 20:12). After 40 years of wandering around in circles in the wilderness with the

Israelites until the first generation of rebellious ex-slaves died off (disinheritance) — all except Joshua and Caleb, who had been faithful to God's promise of inheritance (Numbers 14) — Moses would not personally be allowed to cross over into the promised land. He would not personally inherit his portion of the land. (As a Levite [Exodus 2:1], he could not own rural land permanently, but he could lawfully own property in the Levitical cities [Leviticus 25:32-33].)

The true saint finishes what he begins. Finishing one's assigned task is what counts. This is even more important than what you initially say you will do. Jesus said to the chief priests of the temple and the elders:

> But what think ye? A certain man had two sons; and he came to the first, and said, Son, go work to day in my vineyard. He answered and said, I will not: but afterward he repented, and went. And he came to the second, and said likewise. And he answered and said, I go, sir: and went not. Whether of them twain did the will of his father? They say unto him, The first. Jesus saith unto them, Verily I say unto you, That the publicans and the harlots go into the kingdom of God before you. For John came unto you in the way of righteousness, and ye believed him not: but the publicans and the harlots believed him: and ye, when ye had seen it, repented not afterward, that ye might believe him (Matthew 21:28-32).

If a protest is righteous, the faithful saints will come. Even if they say initially that they will not come, eventually they do come. There were no waves of protest from Protestant Christians when the U.S. Supreme Court handed down the *Roe v. Wade* decision in January of 1973. It took several years after *Roe v. Wade* before Christians, especially Protestant Christians, began to figure out what is really involved in publicly sanctioned abortion: murder, covenantal faithlessness, and the threat of God's visible wrath. Even today, only a comparative handful of Christians have even bothered to picket local abortion centers. But the saints will persevere. The first son, who initially says no, will eventually show up for duty. He is the true heir.

But the longer he waits, the higher his costs. By the time he shows up, the confrontation will have elevated. He will have to serve in a far riskier war. There will be others who have served their time in the trenches and will have marched ahead. On the other hand, there will be some who have grown weary of the struggle and have gone home. But history does not march backward. The escalation will continue.

This fact frightens those Christians who do not want to bear personal responsibility as the representative agents of the covenanted corporate fellowship of Christians. Some will retreat silently, leaving the battlefield altogether. Others will retreat and call it true service, with the official excuse that the confrontation is now illegitimate because it has escalated. (Where did they think confrontation over a literal life-and-death issue would lead? Did they imagine that the abortion question would be settled in the peaceful surroundings of a church supper?) These defections in the name of a supposedly "higher moral vision" make it more difficult for those who delayed joining the fight from the early stages. But, on the other hand, the very nature of the higher risks will attract the more dedicated people.

It will also attract fanatics on both sides who lack personal self-discipline, which is why I outlined some basic organizational screening devices to remove them before they bring shame on the protest (see Chapter 3, subsection on "Self-Government Under Biblical Law.")

If there are few saints who actually do appear for duty in the literal life-and-death battle over abortion, then God will surely disinherit this generation, just as He disinherited the Jews of the Northern Kingdom of Israel when He raised up the Assyrians to scatter them, and when He raised up Babylon to capture Judah over a century later.

Whose Discontinuity: Satan's or God's?

We begin with Satan's discontinuity. When Satan came to Eve

and tempted her, he sought to destroy God's continuity of inheritance. If he could get Eve to disobey God, and if Eve would then lure Adam into disobedience, then Satan could gain the inheritance of the world, at least temporarily. By disobeying God, Eve and then Adam would come under Satan's covenantal rule. "No man can serve two masters," Jesus said, "for either he will hate the one, and love the other; or else he will hold to the one, and despise the other. Ye cannot serve God and mammon" (Matthew 6:24). Satan knew this and acted in terms of it. He understood that Adam's disobedience to God's law would break the covenant between God and man. It would lead to man's disinheritance.

Disinheritance in the Bible is covenantal, but it is ultimately *disinheritance by execution.* God had warned Adam that "in the day that thou eatest thereof thou shalt surely die" (Genesis 2:17b). The sanction of disinheritance is a preliminary down payment on the future death sentence.

We have to understand the biblical meaning of inheritance. Paul wrote in Ephesians:

> That in the dispensation of the fulness of times he might gather together in one all things in Christ, both which are in heaven, and which are on earth; even in him: In whom also we have obtained an inheritance, being predestinated according to the purpose of him who worketh all things after the counsel of his own will: That we should be to the praise of his glory, who first trusted in Christ. In whom ye also trusted, after that ye heard the word of truth, the gospel of your salvation: in whom also after that ye believed, ye were sealed with that holy Spirit of promise, Which is the earnest of our inheritance until the redemption of the purchased possession, unto the praise of his glory (Ephesians 1:10-14).

It has always been Satan's goal to thwart this plan by getting God's children — Adam and Eve originally, and God's covenantally adopted children (John 1:12) subsequently — to break their covenant with God through ethical rebellion. Thus, he seeks to provoke men to break the covenant through disobedience. To put it another way, Satan seeks to provoke a revolution by means of an ethical discontinuity. This means revolution through covenant-breaking.

God's Discontinuity

How does God restore the discontinuity between Him and His children? How does he heal the breach — a covenantal breach? He does it by means of an even greater discontinuity: the covenantal break at Calvary between Him and His Son, Jesus Christ. "And about the ninth hour Jesus cried with a loud voice, saying, Eli, Eli, lama sabachthani? that is to say, My God, my God, why hast thou forsaken me?" (Matthew 27:46). *God disinherited His Son, Jesus Christ, so that He might adopt His lost children, the children of Adam.* God the Father had to execute His Son Jesus Christ. Why? Because there can be no covenantal disinheritance without the death of the disinherited heir. Only the death of God's Son could meet this demand, for Jesus Christ became the One through whom God's adopted children might inherit.

Thus, Jesus Christ served as both the sacrificial lamb and the sacrificing high priest, as the Son who died and also as the Testator who died. This dual role of Jesus Christ is taught specifically by the Epistle to the Hebrews:

> For if the blood of bulls and of goats, and the ashes of an heifer sprinkling the unclean, sanctifieth to the purifying of the flesh: How much more shall the blood of Christ, who through the eternal Spirit offered himself without spot to God, purge your conscience from dead works to serve the living God? And for this cause he is the mediator of the new testament, that by means of death, for the redemption of the transgressions that were under the first testament, they which are called might receive the promise of eternal inheritance. For where a testament is, there must also of necessity be the death of the testator. For a testament is of force after men are dead: otherwise it is of no strength at all while the testator liveth. Whereupon neither the first testament was dedicated without blood. For when Moses had spoken every precept to all the people according to the law, he took the blood of calves and of goats, with water, and scarlet wool, and hyssop, and sprinkled both

the book, and all the people, Saying, This is the blood of the testament which God hath enjoined unto you (Hebrews 9:13-20).

For Christ is not entered into the holy places made with hands, which are the figures of the true; but into heaven itself, now to appear in the presence of God for us: Nor yet that he should offer himself often, as the high priest entereth into the holy place every year with blood of others; For then must he often have suffered since the foundation of the world: but now once in the end of the world hath he appeared to put away sin by the sacrifice of himself. And as it is appointed unto men once to die, but after this the judgment: So Christ was once offered to bear the sins of many; and unto them that look for him shall he appear the second time without sin unto salvation (Hebrews 9:24-28).

God has reestablished covenantal continuity with His people by means of this ultimate discontinuity, the death of His Son. This discontinuity cannot be broken once it is established. Nothing can separate us from the love of God. Nothing can separate us from our inheritance.

And we know that all things work together for good to them that love God, to them who are the called according to his purpose. For whom he did foreknow, he also did predestinate to be conformed to the image of his Son, that he might be the firstborn among many brethren. Moreover whom he did predestinate, them he also called: and whom he called, them he also justified: and whom he justified, them he also glorified. What shall we then say to these things? If God be for us, who can be against us? He that spared not his own Son, but delivered him up for us all, how shall he not with him also freely give us all things? Who shall lay any thing to the charge of God's elect? It is God that justifieth. Who is he that condemneth? It is Christ that died, yea rather, that is risen again, who is even at the right hand of God, who also maketh intercession for us. Who shall separate us from the love of Christ? shall tribulation, or distress, or persecution, or famine, or nakedness, or peril, or sword? As it is written, For thy sake we are killed all the day long; we are accounted as sheep for the slaughter. Nay, in all these things we are more than conquerors through him that loved us. For I am persuaded, that neither death, nor life, nor angels, nor principalities, nor powers, nor things present, nor things to come, Nor height, nor depth, nor any other creature, shall be able to separate us from the love of God, which is in Christ Jesus our Lord (Romans 8:28-39).

In short, the discontinuity introduced in history by Satan is overcome in Jesus Christ. Thus, it is the Christian's God-assigned task to preach the gospel of reconciliation, both in word and deed, to the lost. The great discontinuity is forever behind us: the death of Jesus Christ.

Whose Continuity: Satan's or God's?

Satan seeks to defend his kingdom. He seeks to get men to worship him by failing to worship God. This was the essence of his temptation of Jesus in the wilderness. "Again, the devil taketh him up into an exceeding high mountain, and sheweth him all the kingdoms of the world, and the glory of them; And saith unto him, All these things will I give thee, if thou wilt fall down and worship me. Then saith Jesus unto him, Get thee hence, Satan: for it is written, Thou shalt worship the Lord thy God, and him only shalt thou serve" (Matthew 4:8-10). Satan sought to lure Jesus into Adam's original discontinuity by tempting Him to rebel against God. This strategy failed.

Satan seeks to maintain man's *continuity of rebellion against God*. He has captured his kingdom through Adam's rebellion. He now occupies it as a squatter occupies unclaimed or stolen land. He can retain control over this domain only by getting the sons of Adam to acknowledge his title to the inheritance. This is why the great discontinuity of the crucifixion of Christ now threatens his kingdom. That discontinuity re-established the original covenantal continuity between God and redeemed mankind.

The continuity of covenant-breaking man's rebellion is threatened by God's free offer of the gospel. Those who accept the offer of the gospel break their existing covenant with Satan. They establish a covenantal continuity with God by means of soul-saving faith in Jesus Christ. This is what it means to be "born again" or "born from above." It is a legal act of *adoption*. A person moves from the family of the first Adam to the family of the last Adam. He moves from inheritance with Satan to inheritance with Christ.

What is Satan's inheritance? "Then shall he say also unto them on the left hand, Depart from me, ye cursed, into everlasting fire, prepared for the devil and his angels" (Matthew 25:41). "And death and hell were cast into the lake of fire. This is the second death. And whosoever was not found written in the book of life was cast into the lake of fire" (Revelation 20:14-15). This is the future discontinuity: separation from God's blessing. This begins a permanent continuity: the eternal wrath of God in the lake of fire: cursing.

God's Continuity

God's continuity is ethical. His Word of law to man establishes His continuity. "Think not that I am come to destroy the law, or the prophets: I am not come to destroy, but to fulfil. For verily I say unto you, Till heaven and earth pass, one jot or one tittle shall in no wise pass from the law, till all be fulfilled. Whosoever therefore shall break one of these least commandments, and shall teach men so, he shall be called the least in the kingdom of heaven: but whosoever shall do and teach them, the same shall be called great in the kingdom of heaven. For I say unto you, That except your righteousness shall exceed the righteousness of the scribes and Pharisees, ye shall in no case enter into the kingdom of heaven" (Matthew 5:17-20).

When Christians take seriously God's law, they place themselves visibly inside His covenant. This is a visible testimony to other men regarding the covenantal faithfulness of God.

Ye are the salt of the earth: but if the salt have lost his savour, wherewith shall it be salted? It is thenceforth good for nothing, but to be cast out, and to be trodden under foot of men. Ye are the light of the world. A city that is set on an hill cannot be hid. Neither do men light a candle, and put it under a bushel, but on a candlestick;

and it giveth light unto all that are in the house. Let your light so shine before men, that they may see your good works, and glorify your Father which is in heaven (Matthew 5:13-16).

It is this *continuity of obedience* that is the essence of a Christian's kingdom citizenship.

And hereby we do know that we know him, if we keep his commandments. He that saith, I know him, and keepeth not his commandments, is a liar, and the truth is not in him. (I John 2:3-4).

And whatsoever we ask, we receive of him, because we keep his commandments, and do those things that are pleasing in his sight (I John 3:22).

And he that keepeth his commandments dwelleth in him, and he in him. And hereby we know that he abideth in us, by the Spirit which he hath given us (I John 3:24).

By this we know that we love the children of God, when we love God, and keep his commandments. For this is the love of God, that we keep his commandments: and his commandments are not grievous. (I John 5:2-3).

And this is love, that we walk after his commandments. This is the commandment, That, as ye have heard from the beginning, ye should walk in it (II John 1:6).

Blessed are they that do his commandments, that they may have right to the tree of life, and may enter in through the gates into the city (Revelation 22:14).

Discontinuity and Continuity in Each Kingdom

Who then is the true revolutionary? The person who peaceably obeys the laws of Satan's kingdom, or the person who resists?

Satan calls the person who freely obeys his representatives a law-abiding citizen. God calls the person who freely obeys Satan's representatives a covenant-breaker. Satan calls a person who resists his representatives a revolutionary. God calls a person who resists Satan's representatives a covenant-keeper.

So, whose definition of "law-abiding citizen" should a Christian accept? Satan's or God's? Whose definition of "revolutionary" should a Christian accept? Satan's or God's?

It ought to be clear by now whose definitions are covenantally binding: God's. Thus, when we seek to discover which course of action is morally binding on us, we should seek first to discover God's definitions and descriptions of moral, covenant-keeping behavior. We should not allow Satan's civil representatives to define our categories for us. We should look to God's definitions for guidance. There are no common definitions, any more than there are common principles of civil law. There are God's definitions and God's law. We begin with these. It is the myth of humanism that anything on earth or in heaven is neutral. Everything is covenantal. Nothing is neutral.

Breaking With Satan

There must be a fundamental break with Satan in the life of every Christian. This is the discontinuity described in the Bible as the transition *from wrath to grace* or *from death to life*. If it is to become eternally binding, this transition must be made in each person's days on earth. "The Father loveth the Son, and hath given all things into his hand. He that believeth on the Son hath everlasting life: and he that believeth not the Son shall not see life; but the wrath of God abideth on him" (John 3:35-36).

This fundamental break is supposed to be visible in the life of each Christian. Therefore, *with respect to Satan's kingdom*, each Christian becomes a revolutionary at the point of his conversion. He breaks his covenant with Satan and establishes it with God. Rahab did this when she became treasonous to Jericho by making a covenant with the spies (Joshua 2). To make the covenant with God she had to become treasonous to Jericho. This was the same covenantal act. To claim her inheritance with God's covenant people she necessarily had to renounce her inheritance with Jericho. She did this symbolically by placing the scarlet thread in her window (Joshua 2:18-19).

Rahab became a righteous revolutionary. She had no choice, once she had decided to covenant with Israel's future through the spies. She revolted against Satan's kingdom. This is inescapable for anyone who covenants to God's kingdom.

It is astounding that Christians are not informed of the revolutionary implications of conversion, either before or after making a profession of faith in Jesus Christ as Lord and Savior. There is almost a kind of embarrassment on the part of soul-winners to tell people the radical nature of making a profession of faith in Jesus Christ. It is almost as if the soul-winning techniques are designed to soften the radical distinction between saved and lost, covenant-keeping and covenant-breaking. The potential convert is being asked to make a clean and permanent break with everything evil in his past, yet this is all too frequently downplayed in the presentation of the gospel.

Then the convert matures. He begins to see that this break with evil is definitive. He recognizes as time goes on that he must break publicly and systematically with evil. In short, *he must make public his born-against status as a revolutionary against Satan's kingdom.* Yet as he steadily makes this break visible, he is warned by fellow Christians that he is "going too far." He is "becoming a fanatic." More to the point, *he is becoming an embarrassment to those who have not yet matured in the faith as far as he has.* His visible covenantal faithfulness is a disturbing testimony against their own continuing compromises with evil.

This is what the battle over abortion is all about: extending the revolution of Christ's kingdom against Satan's kingdom. Yet there are many Christians who are afraid of the word "revolution." They are afraid of public confrontations with evil. Why? Because they are still immature in the faith.

Conclusion

There is an inheritance promised by both Satan and God. Satan lies about his inheritance. He offered Jesus Christ the kingdoms of this world, when in fact he possessed no lawful title to any aspect of this world. God, on the other hand, tells the truth about the nature of His inheritance. He tells us that this is His world, and that we have become fellow heirs with Christ. Heirship in God's family is covenantal: by *adoption*. It is therefore also *ethical*.

> For as many as are led by the Spirit of God, they are the sons of God. For ye have not received the spirit of bondage again to fear; but ye have received the Spirit of adoption, whereby we cry, Abba, Father. The Spirit itself beareth witness with our spirit, that we are the children of God: And if children, then heirs; heirs of God, and joint heirs with Christ; if so be that we suffer with him, that we may be also glorified together (Romans 8:14-17).

> Not by works of righteousness which we have done, but according to his mercy he saved us, by the washing of regeneration, and renewing of the Holy Ghost; Which he shed on us abundantly through Jesus Christ our Saviour; That being justified by his grace, we should be made heirs according to the hope of eternal life. This is a faithful saying, and these things I will that thou affirm constantly, that they which have believed in God might be careful to maintain good works. These things are good and profitable unto men (Titus 3:5-8).

Satan hates this view of the kingdom. He hates man. He wants to inherit through the death of man. When Adam died, Satan thought that he would inherit. Instead, Christ through faithfulness even unto death inherited, and spoiled — collected the spoils of war from — Satan's kingdom: "And having spoiled principalities and powers, he made a shew of them openly, triumphing over them in it" (Colossians 2:15).

Satan is the great promoter of abortion. He delights in destroying man's inheritance. He is at war with life. God says, "All those who hate me love death" (Proverbs 8:36b). Satan hates God, and Satan loves death, especially the death of man. Thus, we should not be surprised to see the battle for the soul of the modern world being fought over the abortion question. It will never be settled until Satan's kingdom is obliterated.

Christians must become consistent with their religious presuppositions. They must affirm the right to life. They must commit personally and publicly to the principle that execution is only legitimate for criminals convicted in a court of law for a biblically defined capital crime. Anything else is murder.

If Satan persuades Christians to retreat from this fight, then he will have brought God's sanctions onto the heads of those who became the apologists for abortion. But covenant-keepers may suffer in the period of judgment, just as Jeremiah and Ezekiel went into the Babylonian captivity.

God is not mocked.

In summary:

1. Christian protesters are called revolutionaries by non-protesting Christians.

2. Revolution is a discontinuous disruption in history.

3. The Bible teaches that social continuity is God's gift to those societies that are covenantally faithful: inheritance.

4. A revolution against evil is a curse from God: disinheritance.

5. Evil-doers get a few generations to repent or to compound their evil.

6. They are cut off in history if they persist in their evil.

7. God grants long-term peace to covenant-keeping societies.

8. The saints persevere.

9. A saint is someone who has legal access to God's sanctuary.

10. He is God's counsellor, just as Moses was.

11. Moses appealed to covenant promises: continuity.

12. The true saint finishes what he begins.

13. If a protest is righteous, it will draw righteous followers.

14. This sometimes takes many years (*Roe v. Wade*).

15. The longer a righteous person waits, the higher the costs.

16. Protests escalate over time: greater risk.

17. Fanatics on both sides are also attracted as the protest escalates.

18. God will disinherit a society that allows public evil to escalate unopposed.

19. Satan's revolution was a discontinuity against righteousness.

20. Adam was disinherited by execution.

21. God the Father restores righteous continuity with the ultimate discontinuity: the crucifixion of Jesus Christ.

22. This re-established continuity is unbreakable.

23. Satan seeks a continuity of evil.

24. The gospel's ethical discontinuity (adoption) threatens Satan's continuity.

25. Satan is progressively disinherited as God's regenerating grace spreads.

26. God's continuity is ethical: biblical law.

27. Covenant-keepers affirm a continuity of obedience.

28. The true revolutionary is the one who seeks to maintain the continuity of Satan's evil reign.

29. The true counter-revolutionary is the one who brings Christ's discontinuous gospel to the lost.

30. The discontinuity of the gospel is from wrath to grace, from death to life.

31. Rahab was a righteous revolutionary.

32. Conversion is a revolutionary act against the continuity of evil.

33. Both Satan and God offer an inheritance.

34. Satan lies about his offer.

35. Satan hates man and hates life.

36. Satan is the great promoter of abortion: the death of man.

CONCLUSION

Ye are the salt of the earth: but if the salt have lost his savour, wherewith shall it be salted? it is thenceforth good for nothing, but to be cast out, and to be trodden under foot of men (Matthew 5:13).

For every one shall be salted with fire, and every sacrifice shall be salted with salt. Salt is good: but if the salt have lost his saltness, wherewith will ye season it? Have salt in yourselves, and have peace one with another (Mark 9:49-50).

Salt is good: but if the salt have lost his savour, wherewith shall it be seasoned? It is neither fit for the land, nor yet for the dunghill; but men cast it out. He that hath ears to hear, let him hear (Luke 14:34-35).

What is salt good for? Three things. First, it adds flavor to food. Second, it serves as a preservative. Both of these uses are blessings. Third, it destroys the productivity of the land. "And that the whole land thereof is brimstone, and salt, and burning, that it is not sown, nor beareth, nor any grass groweth therein, like the overthrow of Sodom, and Gomorrah, Admah, and Zeboim, which the LORD overthrew in his anger, and in his wrath" (Deuteronomy 29:23). It is therefore a tool of judgment: God's negative sanction. Salting over a city was a strategy of military conquest in the ancient world. "And Abimelech fought against the city all that day; and he took the city, and slew the people that was therein, and beat down the city, and sowed it with salt" (Judges 9:45).

Most people think of the first use of salt. A few may think of

120

the second. Almost nobody thinks of the third. That is the problem today: nobody wants to think of God's permanent sanctions, not even Christians.

The Old Testament required salt in the sacrifices. "And every oblation of thy meat offering shalt thou season with salt; neither shalt thou suffer the salt of the covenant of thy God to be lacking from thy meat offering: with all thine offerings thou shalt offer salt (Leviticus 2:13). The sacrifices symbolized the burning flesh of the lake of fire. God allowed the sacrifices of animals to serve as symbolic substitutes for man. God's covenant requires salt. "All the heave offerings of the holy things, which the children of Israel offer unto the LORD, have I given thee, and thy sons and thy daughters with thee, by a statute for ever: it is a covenant of salt for ever before the LORD unto thee and to thy seed with thee" (Numbers 18:19).

Today, abortionists use a saline (salt) solution that is injected into the mother's uterus. The solution literally burns the baby to death. The abortionist has selected a means of destroying the innocent that testifies to the abortionists' own eternal future, as well as the mother's. This is Satan's imitation covenant, a covenant of death.

Christians are called to be the salt of the earth: flavoring, preserving, and destroying. Salt is covenantal. Christians are required by God to honor the terms of His covenant. They are to act in his name (point two), in terms of his law (point three), bringing His sanctions in history — blessing and cursing (point four), extending His kingdom in history, while simultaneously salting over Satan's kingdom (point five).

The trouble is, Christians are unfamiliar with these tasks. They have not been taught the essentials of covenant theology. They do not understand the comprehensive nature of the gospel. They do not know what it means to be God's salt in history. They barely understand point one of the covenant: the doctrine of God.

Transcendence and Presence in
Progressive Sanctification

God the Creator and Judge is wholly transcendent to this world, yet He is always present with His people. If He were not totally transcendent to this world, He would be neither its Creator nor its Judge. On the other hand, if He were not present with this world, He could not influence its development. He would be bound by a self-imposed "hands off" policy. The hypothetical god of eighteenth-century Deism — transcendence without presence — was so distant from his creation as to pay no attention to the world and to leave it entirely alone. He just "wound the world up" like a clock and departed. In contrast, the hypothetical god of pantheism — presence without transcendence — is so much a part of this world that he cannot bring it under judgment. He is incapable of changing it because he is immersed in it. Covenant-breaking man is willing to accept either of these two false gods in preference to the true God of the Bible.

What is true of God is analogically true of Christians. This is why we need a biblical definition of God: wholly transcendent, yet personally present. If we were not linked covenantally to a transcendent God, then we would have no legal authority as His designated representatives to call other men to account in God's name. On the other hand, if God were not present with us in our various callings and tasks, we could not change the world because we would be neither of the world nor in it. But we are in this world, set apart (sanctified) as *saints*, and therefore burdened with the God-given responsibility of *calling this world to account* and also *working from within to change it*. We are not of this world because we are linked to a transcendent God by means of His covenant, and this covenantal bond defines us, not our present geographical and temporal location. At the same time, we also are in the world as His covenantal agents. Jesus made this clear in His public prayer before God:

> And all mine are thine, and thine are mine; and I am glorified in them. And now I am no more in the world, but these are in the

world, and I come to thee. Holy Father, keep through thine own
name those whom thou hast given me, that they may be one, as
we are. While I was with them in the world, I kept them in thy
name: those that thou gavest me I have kept, and none of them is
lost, but the son of perdition; that the scripture might be fulfilled.
And now come I to thee; and these things I speak in the world,
that they might have my joy fulfilled in themselves. I have given
them thy word; and the world hath hated them, because they are
not of the world, even as I am not of the world. I pray not that
thou shouldest take them out of the world, but that thou shouldest
keep them from the evil. They are not of the world, even as I am
not of the world. Sanctify them through thy truth: thy word is
truth. As thou hast sent me into the world, even so have I also sent
them into the world. And for their sakes I sanctify myself, that they
also might be sanctified through the truth (John 17:10-19).

This process of personal progressive sanctification – setting
oneself aside more and more for God's service throughout one's
lifetime – is each Christian's God-assigned task. We are required
by God to set ourselves apart from the sins of this world, step by
step, year by year. This is not a process of withdrawal from this
world. Jesus made this plain: "I pray not that thou shouldest take
them out of the world, but that thou shouldest keep them from the
evil." But if we are not to be removed from this world, yet we are
also to be set apart from Satan, how can we do this? There is only
one way: *we must progressively extend the kingdom of God in history*
through the preaching of the gospel and the subduing of all things
to God's glory in terms of His revealed ethical standards.

Reconciliation

We are not to be reconciled to this sin-filled world. The gospel
nevertheless is a message of reconciliation. It obviously has to be
a message of reconciling this world to God through the ethical
transformation of men and institutions.

And all things are of God, who hath reconciled us to himself
by Jesus Christ, and hath given to us the ministry of reconciliation;
To wit, that God was in Christ, reconciling the world unto himself,

not imputing their trespasses unto them; and hath committed unto
us the word of reconciliation (I Corinthians 5:18-19).

Wherefore in all things it behoved him to be made like unto
his brethren, that he might be a merciful and faithful high priest
in things pertaining to God, to make reconciliation for the sins of
the people (Hebrews 2:17).

And, having made peace through the blood of his cross, by him
to reconcile all things unto himself; by him, I say, whether they be
things in earth, or things in heaven. And you, that were sometime
alienated and enemies in your mind by wicked works, yet now hath
he reconciled in the body of his flesh through death, to present you
holy and unblamable and unreproveable in his sight (Colossians
1:20-22).

This process of cultural reconciliation inevitably is also a
process of *covenantal confrontation*. Whatever is not reconciled to God
through Jesus Christ is to be *subdued* — at the final judgment
surely, but also in history. Sin's power of rebellion is to be weak-
ened. Christianity provides the cultural standards by which the
rebellious world is to be brought under God's dominion. Thus,
Christians are not to limit their efforts to personal sanctification;
they must also work to extend cultural and institutional sanctification. Like salt, they are to flavor the good, preserve the good, and
destroy the evil.

How can this be done? The old political slogan is true: **"You
can't beat something with nothing!"** Christians must therefore
offer something better in every area of life. Wherever sin has
tarnished man's institutions — obviously, this means everywhere — the healing gospel of salvation is to overcome the effects
of sin.

The Speed of Social Transformation

This transformation cannot be accomplished overnight. It is
the product of the steady extension of God's law through the
empowering of the Holy Spirit. This healing of man's institutions,
like the healing of individuals, is progressive. It takes place over

time. It takes place over many generations, as the third commandment says, as God shows His mercy "unto thousands [of generations] of them that love me, and keep my commandments" (Exodus 20:6). In this sense, *Christianity is anti-Revolutionary.* It preaches the doctrine of regeneration through time.

Nevertheless, Christianity also teaches the moral necessity of confrontation and resistance against evil — evil thoughts, evil acts, evil men, and evil institutions. Christianity's long-term earthly goal is to reduce the influence of evil in every area of life. Therefore, its long-term cultural goal is to reduce the influence of public evil in every area of life.

The more publicly evil the social environment the Christian lives in, the more revolutionary the personal transformation of conversion is. At the same time, the less the new convert can do to change things. This is analogous to the doctrine of transcendence: the covenantal break at the time of personal conversion to Christ is so great that the convert is left with little that he can do to extend his faith to the institutional world around him. His reaction to his environment must be primarily defensive. This is what Christians face in prison camps or in the national prisons we call Communist nations.

The less publicly evil the social environment, the more points of contact the new convert can have with it. The more places that he can confront it publicly and begin to change it. It is more like the doctrine of presence: the convert is more present in the day-to-day operations of his institutional world. He can work to change his social environment's public face precisely because it has not yet departed into more fully self-consistent iniquity. This is what Christians face in the Industrial West.

Thus we face a peculiar anomaly. In those social environments in which Christianity represents a more revolutionary public break, Christians are forced to be very circumspect and very conservative in order to stay out of jail. They operate under a far more restricted legal and political environment. Thus, they must "go underground" in many of their activities: worship, baptisms, and evangelism.

They know that it will take many generations of personal and ecclesiastical covenantal faithfulness for the leaven of righteousness to transform their culture.

In contrast, within those social environments in which Christianity represents a less revolutionary public break, Christians are enabled to become more confrontational and more visibly radical. They operate under a far more open legal and political environment. Thus, they face few restrictions on conducting the basics of the faith — worship, baptisms, evangelism — and have resources and time remaining for conducting visible challenges to the sin-filled social order.

This produces a seemingly strange pair of phenomena. First, those who are in principle most alienated from their social environment will be least visibly in rebellion against it. The tactics of Christian resistance require a much lower profile, analogous to the Hebrew midwives. Second, converts who are closer culturally to their not equally corrupted social environment — *assuming they take seriously the challenge of God's dominion mandate to subdue the earth* (Genesis 1:26-28; 9:1-17) — will appear to be far more visibly in rebellion against their society.

You would think, then, that Christians in the United States and the Industrial West would be far more visibly confrontational. They have greater freedom to confront evil. But this has not been true for over a century. Why?

The Paralysis of Pietism

The reason why American Christianity seems so docile publicly is not because America is a self-conscious anti-Christian tyranny but rather because of the world-rejecting effects of traditional American Protestant pietism. This view of life teaches at least three things:

1. This world cannot be progressively brought into conformity to God's social standards because a) there is insufficient time to reform the world's institutions, and b) the Holy Spirit will never

perform anything like the worldwide transformation of men's hearts.

2. The biblical concept of progressive sanctification is therefore limited to the individual soul, the family, and the local church.

3. The mark of personal holiness is withdrawal from the cultural, political, and social affairs of this world.

This outlook is analogous to the heresy of Deism. The Deist god is so far removed from the creation that he does not call it to repentance; He does not bring sanctions in history. Similarly, the pietist is "so heavenly minded that he is of no earthly good." Because Christians have not had a biblical concept of transcendence — the absolute sovereignty of God — they have adopted an implicitly Deistic concept of God's transcendence, and therefore Christian man's covenantal distance from this world.

Because the modern Christian's doctrine of God's transcendence is incorrect because it is not grounded in the doctrine of the covenant, so is his doctrine of God's presence. His view of civilization is closer to pantheism's view than he wants to admit. The defeatist cultural outlook of pietism is also analogous to the heresy of pantheism. The pantheist sees god as so immersed in the creation that he cannot change it. Similarly, the pietist sees the Christian as so dependent on his culture that he cannot expect to change it. He is impotent to make a significant cultural difference. He surrenders history to Satan and his covenantal agents. He abandons earthly hope. I am not exaggerating. Listen to pietist theologian Lehman Strauss on his assessment of the modern world, in an article titled, "Our Only Hope":

> We are witnessing in this twentieth century the collapse of civilization. It is obvious that we are advancing toward the end of the age. Science can offer no hope for the future blessing and security of humanity, but instead it has produced devastating and deadly results which threaten to lead us toward a new dark age. The frightful uprisings among races, the almost unbelievable conquests of Communism, and the growing antireligious philosophy throughout the world, all spell out the fact that doom is certain. I

can see no bright prospects, through the efforts of man, for the earth and its inhabitants. [Lehman Strauss, "Our Only Hope," *Bibliotheca Sacra*, Vol. 120 (April/June 1963), p. 154.]

This culturally pessimistic outlook of "no earthly hope in the 'Church Age'" has dominated American fundamentalism for over a century. American Protestant Christianity for about a century was socially and politically invisible as an independent influence. The abortion issue has now begun to break this strangle hold of eschatological pessimism and social paralysis. There is no question that Christians are at the forefront of this social protest movement. This makes a lot of Christian leaders nervous. They see where it could lead, namely, to a transformation of the American evangelical consciousness: *from pietism to activism.* It could also lead to a shift in eschatology: *from premillennialism to postmillennialism.* But most important, it could (and I believe will) lead to a shift in moral theology: *from natural law to biblical law.*

Natural Law Theology and Political Pluralism

Modern culture says that abortion is morally valid; anti-abortionist Christians know that it is not. There is no way to reconcile these two positions. There is no halfway house between abortion and birth. Thus, anti-abortionist Christians have begun to call into question the intellectual foundation of the American churches' long compromise with paganism: natural law theology. By standing in the doorways of murderers, and by breaking the civil law of trespassing, they have openly begun to break with the political philosophy of pluralism, the idea that every person's view should have the opportunity of becoming the law of the land. God grants no such political right to abortionists. Why, then, should Christians acknowledge as valid any political philosophy that says that God does grant such rights to abortionists?

Operation Rescue is calling people to the non-violent barricades. The act of physical interposition is clearly the Christian's first step — probably not a self-conscious step — in the philosophical war against political pluralism. Christian leaders can see where these protests may be headed, even if their followers cannot: to a total confrontation with the civilization of secular humanism. Such a total confrontation requires a consistent, thoroughly developed theology to defend it and implement it. After all, you can't beat something with nothing. There is only one possible choice today: *covenant theology*. After the protesters have read this book, and have accepted its conclusions, they may decide to read my other book, which I am writing at the same time: *Political Polytheism: The Myth of Pluralism* (Institute for Christian Economics, 1989). This, too, makes Christian leaders very nervous.

These theological and political implications of non-violent Christian interposition may be why so few Christian leaders have become vocal supporters of Operation Rescue, and why those who have may back down when the theological and political implications of Operation Rescue become clearer (such as with the publication of this book). It will be interesting to see which is their greater enemy: murdering babies or covenant theology.

The Polarizing Issue of Abortion

When the anti-abortion movement escalated, it produced a major breach in traditional American fundamentalism and evangelicalism. The world-retreating, confrontation-avoiding pietists resented the appearance of Christian concern regarding a social and legal issue that is inescapably political. It is one thing to send money to a local rescue mission to help sober up drunks. It is something else again to get involved in political action to make illegal a now-socially acceptable form of murder, as abortion had been throughout American history prior to 1973. This is why Francis Schaeffer wrote *The Great Evangelical Disaster*: to warn evangelicals of the moral evil of deliberately remaining on the sidelines of life when society faces a literal life-and-death issue.

Abortion has been regarded as a sin throughout the history of the church, but this does not faze the pietists, since they do not know much about church history, and they regard church history as mostly a series of mistakes. Not seeing the progress of history, including church history, and not seeing progress even in the church's creeds in history, they are not impressed by appeals to history.

The anti-abortion movement has now begun to force the hands of Christians. As C. S. Lewis said, as time rolls on, the moral constraints on men are restricting their mobility of decision-making. The moral issues are getting clearer. Each side of the theological war becomes more consistent with its own viewpoint and therefore has less freedom of decision-making. The confrontation inevitably escalates as time goes on.

Hostility to Confrontation

There are lots of arguments possible against the idea of the legitimacy of Christian resistance. Men can deny that Old Testament law or Old Testament examples are morally or legally binding on Christians today. This leaves them with almost no God-revealed authoritative standards on anything outside of family and church matters. Those who are entering the battle against abortion or any other major conflict between humanism and Christianity disarm themselves if they adopt such a view of the Old Testament's irrelevance in New Testament times.

Another argument is that non-violent resistance is illegitimate unless authorized by a lower magistrate. To which I ask: What about freedom of the press, freedom of speech, and freedom of calling evil men to account? Presbyterian minister Samuel Rutherford in 1644 published his defense of biblical law and the right of resistance to tyrants, *Lex, Rex*. It defended the traditional Calvinist position that in order to justify taking up arms against the state, a lesser magistrate must approve the rebellion. He died in 1661, the year after Charles II, the anti-Puritan king of England, returned to the throne. The government regarded his book as "inveighing against monarchie and laying ground for rebellion," and ordered every copy burned. Anyone owning a copy was then treated as an enemy of the government. Rutherford lost his pensions from both church and university. He was ordered to confine himself to his house. He was then summoned to appear before the Parliament at Edinburgh to defend himself against the formal charge of high treason. His biographer remarked in 1827: "It may be easily imagined what his fate would have been had he lived to obey the mandate; but ere the time arrived he was summoned to a far higher than an earthly tribunal."

Now, what if Rutherford had waited until 1660 to publish the manuscript? Would he have been morally required to get the formal approval of a lower magistrate? No? Then why should someone who engages in non-violent bodily interposition in order to help save the life of an unborn child be required to get such permission? What is the difference between writing a treasonous book (as defined by the tyrannical rulers) and standing in a doorway to prevent murder?

It is time to quit playing verbal games. What Francis Schaeffer described as the great evangelical disaster should be abandoned. When Christians turn again to the Bible instead of to the tradition of world-retreating pietism for their answers, they will learn of a God who has called his people to confrontation with evil, generation after generation. Sometimes this confrontation is private, with deception as the means. Sometimes it is physical but non-violent. And sometimes – as in 1776 in the North American colonies – it is political and military. In this last case, the support of the lower magistrate is required.

Questions of Timing

This is a tactical question. No man knows the future. At best, he can guess what the response will be to any specific action. When he organizes his fellow men to confront some perceived evil, he may be acting prematurely. Time will tell. But to oppose his decision in the name of biblical law or biblical principle when one's objection is merely tactical is a misuse of the Bible. Even worse is to attack him because your objection is essentially personal, for example, because he failed to invite you to sit in his "council of elders" when he and his associates first formulated their protest plans. There seems to be more of this sort of "principled protest" going on these days than Christian leaders care to admit.

Christians no doubt will make many tactical errors. For over half a century they have had no practical experience in public confrontations against civil injustice. They were told that even to get involved in such matters is suspicious. "Politics is dirty," they were told. And because Christians stayed out of politics, politics did indeed remain dirty.

Let us not hide our criticisms of another man's tactics behind the language of biblical principle. Such criticisms can be deflated publicly if they are not tied closely to the biblical principle invoked, much to the embarrassment of the critic. If the critic has not done his homework regarding either biblical law or church history, he is doubly vulnerable.

If what we are doing is grounded in biblical principle, or at least not opposed to biblical principle, let us then adhere to the tactician's prime rule of non-violent confrontation:

"The action is the reaction."

Let us plan carefully to get the reactions we need that will gain us support for the next stage in our proposed campaign against public evil.

Appendix A

ARE *OPERATION RESCUE'S* CRITICS SELF-SERVING?

And the princes of Issachar were with Deborah; even Issachar, and also Barak: he was sent on foot into the valley. For the divisions of Reuben there were great thoughts of heart. Why abodest thou among the sheepfolds, to hear the bleatings of the flocks? For the divisions of Reuben there were great searchings of heart. Gilead abode beyond Jordan: and why did Dan remain in ships? Asher continued on the sea shore, and abode in his breaches. Zebulun and Naphtali were a people that jeoparded their lives unto the death in the high places of the field (Judges 5:15-18).

Deborah had issued a challenge to Israel: Come and fight the enemies of God! Some tribes came, but others did not. The tribe of Issachar came, but the tribe of Reuben stayed home, safe among the sheep. They were too busy searching their hearts. Dan went fishing. But Zebulun and Naphtali jeopardized their lives unto death. All this was immortalized by General Deborah in her song.

There are always those who choose to go fishing in the midst of a life-and-death crisis. Christians in Russia did in 1917. Christians in Germany did in 1932. The Dans of this world are legion, especially in the twentieth-century church. But my concern here is not with Dan; it is with Reuben. Dans choose not to get involved, but they are polite enough to remain quiet. They are not deep thinkers.

Not so the Reubenites. They preferred the company of sheep. They were deeply thoughtful — so thoughtful that they never could quite find the time to move away from their bleating sheep. They thought, and thought, and thought. But they did not act. They chose instead to be conformed to the image of their sheep.

These days, unfortunately, the Reubens of this world are not content to sit and think deep thoughts. They all seem to have computers, word processors, and laser printers. Or maybe they have only dot-matrix printers. The point is, they are not content to sit among their sheep, immobilized in thought. They want others to join them in the peaceful sheepfolds. If no one joins them, then they might develop self-doubts about their immobilized condition. They might even wind up in the lyrics of some future song by some contemporary Deborah. And so they issue computer-printed manifestos against the legitimacy of becoming involved in the hard realities of the war.

Sheepfold Manifestos

It is not sufficient for Christians to sit quietly. They see themselves as principled people in an unprincipled social environment. They see themselves as morally different from those around them. And so they feel morally compelled to defend their own inaction by means of selective biblical citations. Thus it has always been. Grand theological schemes justifying not-so-grand personal disengagement can be built from selected Bible texts, once the battle has begun. After all, sheep need looking after. That is what shepherds are for. They need to look after the sheep (and occasionally shear them). I can almost imagine what one of the Reubenite manifestos would have said, had the Reubenites owned word processors and laser printers in the days of Deborah. (Actually, the manifesto would probably have been a sermon that the church secretary typed up for distribution.)

> Who is this Deborah? Who does she think she is? Who put her
> in charge of the armies of Israel? The Bible says that women are
> not to become leaders and elders. When a society has sunk so low

that a woman must lead it, why, it is already under God's curse! The thing we need today is prayer, not women generals. What we need is a great revival, my friends, not needless confrontation with the Amalekites. God has delivered this nation into the hands of the Amalekites for a reason: to show us His great displeasure. Until we get that great revival, we should stay right where we are. God is telling us that it is not yet time to confront Amalekites. This is a time for prayer and fasting — well, anyway, a time for prayer — not political mobilization. So we must do first things first. We must pray. We must hand out gospel tracts. Above all, we must tithe. Dig deep into your wallets, my friends. Jesus wants sacrifice, not vain words and utopian dreams. (Yes, Visa and MasterCard are acceptable in *this* house of God.) Then, when we get enough converts to Christ, certain of us may choose to run for political office. That would be true leadership, not a bunch of women generals. And as soon as enough of us win our elections, we will vote these Amalekites out of the land. "Smite the Amalekites, O Lord! Smite them with voter registration forms!"

The Other Version of Operation Rescue: *The Rapture*

There is a tradition of social inaction in American fundamentalism and evangelical Christianity that stretches back at least to fundamentalism's public relations defeat at the Scopes "monkey trial" in 1925, and really back to the end of the Civil War in 1865. Like battered tortoises, Christians went completely into their shells after 1925. They were shell-shocked into silence for two generations.

Because liberal Christians and the proponents of baptized humanist socialism (the Social Gospel) have long been involved in all sorts of political activism, Bible-believing Christians have tended to equate social and political activism with theological liberalism. Such has not always been the case. Certainly, the American abolitionists of the mid-nineteenth century were mostly Christians, although the national leadership of the abolitionist movement was radical and Unitarian. Before them, the patriots who fought for the American cause in the American Revolution were overwhelmingly Christian. So were the English Puritans of

the 1640's, who launched a successful revolution against a tyrannical, lying king, Charles I. But from 1925, when the Scopes trial
ended in disgrace for William Jennings Bryan and the creationists,
until the mid-1970's, Bible-believing Christians in the United
States fled from any visible corporate responsibility as Christians.
They fled from the intellectual battlefields of life.

Like all those who flee from battle, they sought self-
justification for their cowardice. They developed an entire theology
of Christian cultural impotence in order to justify their visible
absence from the battlefields of life. They told themselves and their
followers that the church of Jesus Christ must and will suffer a
series of inevitable defeats, in every area of life, until things get so
bad that Jesus comes personally to "rapture" Christians out of this
world. This will not be at the end of history at the final judgment,
which Christians have always admitted, but before history is over.
Until that great day — Jesus Christ's supposed version of Operation Rescue — we are told, it is futile to devise grand schemes of
Bible-based social reform. All such hopes and plans must and will
be dashed to bits against the hard rocks of Bible prophecy. This
is the theology of the skid row rescue mission. The best hope it
offers is the possibility of sobering up a handful of drunks before
Jesus comes again.

Some form of the theology of cultural retreat still dominates
most Bible-believing seminaries and pulpits. But it is now starting
to crack. The abortion issue is shaking the foundations of "full-time
Christian non-public service." The great evangelical disaster is
starting to be recognized for the disaster that it is. But it will not
be reversed without a struggle. This struggle can be seen in the
war of the manifestos.

Legalized abortion has now made Christian social irresponsi-
bility appear ridiculous. Thus, we find millions of Christians who
give occasional lip service (and very little money) to the fight
against abortion. We find a small minority willing to picket an
abortion clinic occasionally. We find an even tinier minority ready
to devote regular time and regular money to fighting abortion,

including fighting it politically. And then, in the summer of 1988, a handful of non-violent activists began to "up the ante" by breaking local property laws in Atlanta, Georgia, and later in other cities by interposing their bodies between murderous mothers and their murderous accomplices, state-licensed physicians.

(Strange, isn't it? Liberals for 70 years insisted that "human rights are more important than property rights!" This phrase supposedly proved that high taxes and government regulation of the economy are morally legitimate. But these days, the liberals have spotted a problem with this slogan. A bunch of crazy Christians have started intruding onto the property of wealthy, state-licensed murderers — excuse me, physicians — to interfere with the daily slaughter of the innocents. Now, all of a sudden, the defense of private property is high on the liberals' list of priorities. Liberals certainly enjoy taxing the high incomes of physicians, but they want them to earn those juicy taxable incomes, especially if those incomes come from killing judicially innocent babies. Population control, and all that. And . . . liberals will never actually say this in print, of course . . . these slaughtered babies are mostly blacks and Hispanics. You know. *Those* kind of people! They have concluded that an abortion is less expensive to the welfare state than two decades of aid to a dependent child, but they never say this in public. They think that the cheapest way to "break the cycle of poverty" is to kill the next generation of the potentially poor. And never forget: indigent old people are also part of that cycle.)

Trespassing for Dear Life

This tactic of "trespassing for dear life" has now begun to divide the Christian community. It has already divided Christian leaders. This division appears to cut across denominational and even ideological lines. Christian leaders are being forced to take a position, pro or con, with regard to the legitimacy of this physical interposition. Like Congress, they prefer to avoid taking sides, but the pressures can no longer be avoided easily, at least for Reubenites.

There are two signs in front of abortion clinics:

"No Trespassing"
"Thou Shalt Not Kill"

The "No Trespassing" sign is symbolically stuck into the grass. The "Thou Shalt Not Kill" sign is literally being carried (or ought to be literally carried) by an anti-abortion picketer.

The picketers have now begun to realize that they face a major moral decision: either ignore the implicit "No Trespassing" sign or ignore the covenantal implications of the "Thou Shalt Not Kill" sign. The fact of the matter is that if Christians continue to obey the abortionists' "No Trespassing" signs, God may no longer honor this humanistic nation's "No Trespassing" sign to Him. He will eventually come in national judgment with a vengeance. This is a basic teaching of biblical covenant theology. (It is conveniently ignored in the pseudo-covenant theology of the critics.)

A small, hard core of dedicated Christians has now decided that they cannot obey both signs at the same time. One of these imperatives must be obeyed, and to obey it, the other imperative must be disobeyed. This has precipitated a crisis.

There is a much larger group of Christians that pretends that there is nothing inherently contradictory about these two signs. There is nothing going on behind closed clinic doors that Christians have a moral imperative and judicial authorization from God to get more directly involved in stopping. They prefer not to think about the two signs. They see the first one and assume that it has the highest authority.

There have been other "No Trespassing" signs in history. Outside of German concentration camps in 1943, for instance. But Christians in Germany honored those signs. They forgot the words of Proverbs:

> If thou faint in the day of adversity, thy strength is small. If thou forbear to deliver them that are drawn unto death, and those that are ready to be slain; If thou sayest, Behold, we knew it not; doth not he that pondereth the heart consider it? and he that

keepeth thy soul, doth not he know it? and shall not he render to every man according to his works? (Proverbs 24:10-12).

The Christian critics of physical confrontation have offered many arguments to prove that non-violent interposition by Christians is always morally, legally, and even theologically wrong. Others have argued that it is not always wrong, but it is wrong today.

The critics freely admit, as one of them proclaimed, "After many years of opposing abortion in America, at the cost of millions of dollars and thousands of lives, nothing has changed." This is understated. It has been at the cost of millions of dollars and *tens of millions of lives*. What is his conclusion? That Christians now need to escalate their confrontations, to keep the pressure on? That a decade and a half of peaceful picketing and political mobilization has "tested the judicial waters," and it is now time for Christians to start swimming upstream in order to avoid going over the falls?

No, indeed; rather, he concludes that Christians should now abandon these direct physical confrontations, since peaceful confrontations have proven useless. He does not conclude that lawful confrontations — as the secular humanist state defines lawful — have been useless, but that all confrontations are either useless or counterproductive.

Prayer and preaching are the only things that can work, we are told. Nice, safe, quiet, invisible, publicly acceptable, legal, unindictable prayer and preaching. But not imprecatory psalms, of course. Not prayers from the pulpit that name local abortionists and call down God's visible wrath on their heads. No, just "Dear Jesus, please make everyone sweet and nice, like they were back in 1972, before *Roe v. Wade*. Amen." No otherwise unemployable pastor is going to get himself fired from his upper-middle-class suburban congregation for praying this sort of prayer!

As if the pro-life movement had not been praying and preaching for a decade.

As if the humanists were not preparing an assault on the church as surely as they did in Russia in 1918 and Germany in 1933.

Theology vs. Practice: Growing Schizophrenia

What is remarkable is that some pastors have the rhetorical ability to preach retreat in the face of personal danger as if it were a direct frontal assault against the enemy. They puff up themselves and their rhetoric, pound the pulpit, shout, and generally whoop themselves into a frenzy, as if they were calling their followers into a war, when in fact they are sounding the bugle for "stand pat for Jesus."

What is even more remarkable is that some of them adopt the language of socially victorious postmillennial covenant theology in order to defend the conclusions of traditional retreatist dispensational premillennialism. This takes considerable intellectual skill, I must admit. It is too bad that such skill could not have been put to a more productive use.

Meanwhile, those who have for years said that they believed in the theology of dispensational premillennialism have now adopted an anti-abortion strategy based on the conclusions of traditional postmillennialism: direct social involvement in terms of a victory-oriented strategy. These people are not kamikaze types; they really believe that Christians can and will win this fight.

The abortion issue is cutting across denominational lines and also across theological lines. Which counts for more: theological consistency or righteous action? Obviously, righteous action counts for more. It is not what people say but what they do that counts most in God's eyes.

> But what think ye? A certain man had two sons; and he came to the first, and said, Son, go work to day in my vineyard. He answered and said, I will not: but afterward he repented, and went. And he came to the second, and said likewise. And he answered and said, I go, sir: and went not. Whether of them twain did the will of [his] father? They say unto him, The first. Jesus saith unto

them, Verily I say unto you, That the publicans and the harlots go into the kingdom of God before you. For John came unto you in the way of righteousness, and ye believed him not: but the publicans and the harlots believed him: and ye, when ye had seen it, repented not afterward, that ye might believe him (Matthew 21:28-32).

In my view, this sort of schizophrenia cannot be sustained indefinitely. What people do is more fundamental than what people say. "Yea, a man may say, Thou hast faith, and I have works: shew me thy faith without thy works, and I will shew thee my faith by my works" (James 2:18). As time goes on, people will reshape their theological opinions in terms of their actions. Their theological schizophrenia will be healed by their adoption of a theology that is more consistent with their actions. A man may insist that he is a covenant theologian, but watch what he does. This will tell you where he is headed. Similarly, a man may claim to be a dispensational premillennialist, but watch what he does. This will tell you where he is headed.

The Quality of the Arguments

What about the content, as distinguished from the rhetoric and theology, of these anti-direct confrontation arguments? Not many of these anti-confrontation arguments need to be taken seriously. Most of them are reworked versions of the old 1938 arguments against any form of Christian social involvement. A few, however, are clothed in more modern terminology — "deep social concern" without one iota of personal risk to the "deeply concerned" pastor. Fewer still are serious objections that really do raise serious questions regarding non-violent anti-abortion activism. But they all say basically the same thing: Christians should never break the civil law as individuals who are acting on their own or in unauthorized small groups.

While no Christian would deny that Ehud lawfully killed Moabite King Eglon on his own, institutionally speaking, most Christians would deny that the office of judge still operates today.

I would agree. So, some rationale other than serving as an Old Testament judge must be found to justify non-violent interposition. I have attempted to outline such a defense in this book — a defense based squarely on the biblical covenant model.

I now need to devote space to answering several of the non-covenantal (or imitation covenantal) arguments that have been offered by Christians. I cannot answer all of them. Indeed, it is now the responsibility of the Christian critics of interposition to answer me. I have not tossed out a series of random arguments in this book; I have presented an integrated case based on the biblical covenant model. I am waiting to see something equivalent from anti-confrontational, self-proclaimed covenant theologians — something more persuasive than dot-matrix-printed manifestos. If they remain silent now, then they are admitting that they have no case theologically. To admit this is also to admit that their arguments were designed from the beginning to defend their own personal inaction and the inaction of their churches rather than the product of careful theological investigation.

Too many naive Christians have been persuaded by these sheepfold manifestos with the hidden agendas. They have been bullied theologically into inaction and confusion. Meanwhile, unborn babies are being murdered. It is time for the authors of these manifestos either to answer my book or else reverse or drastically modify their stated position publicly. I think they will do their best to avoid taking any of these steps. To which I respond, in advance: "Theological silence from this point on is not golden; it is yellow."

What the reader must understand is that I am taking every example from published statements from pastors or church officers. I am not making up any of this. These are real arguments — real *stupid* arguments — offered by real men who expect us to take them real seriously.

How seriously should you take these arguments? Decide for yourself. How seriously should you take the people who offered them? Decide for yourself. As you read these objections to Operation Rescue, you need to ask yourself these two questions: 1) If the arguments are truly preposterous, does the manifesto writer have a hidden agenda? 2) What is this hidden agenda?

Abortion Is Not Compulsory

Roe v. Wade is unlike commands by civil rulers requiring citizens to perform evil acts. It does not require that anyone abort her baby.

This is the most imbecilic argument of them all. To see just how ridiculous this argument really is, substitute the word "murder" for "abort." We get the following piece of moral and judicial nonsense: "A law legalizing murder does not require a citizen to murder anyone." Does this make the legalization of murder legitimate? Is a law that legalizes murder anything but perverse? So, what should we call such an argument? Thoughtful?

A civil law does not have to command people to do something evil in order for the law to be evil. Neither the Sanhedrin nor Caesar's representatives commanded the apostles to preach anything evil. They just forbade them from preaching what is true and what is required by God that all Christians preach. So the apostles disobeyed the civil and religious authorities. They knew it was an evil law. They knew that God did not want them to obey it.

Civil laws are almost always framed negatively. They forbid evil acts. They establish punishments for people who commit evil acts. This is the biblical standard for civil law. A mark of the coming of satanic law is when the state starts passing laws that force people to do "good" things. The state has then become messianic, a savior state. Seldom in our day does an evil law bear this mark of Satan: that it commands people to do evil things. *Almost always an evil civil law legalizes something which is evil in itself.* Sometimes an evil law will forbid what is righteous. Rarely will it actually command people to do something immoral.

The abortion laws authorize something evil: murder. Local trespassing laws are now being used to prohibit something righteous: saving judicially innocent lives. The fact that there is no Federal law compelling mothers to abort their children is utterly irrelevant to anything except the hope of confrontation-avoiding Christians that some gullible Christian will take them seriously. Yet Christian authors and pastors offer such an argument as if it were serious. A Christian should suspect the motives of anyone who would deliberately distort reality this badly. I suggest that the critic has a hidden agenda. Nobody comes to conclusions this preposterous without a hidden agenda.

"Pro-Choice" Ethics in "Free Will" Language

> *Does the civil disobedience advocated by Operation Rescue fit the biblical exception [to the general rule against disobeying civil magistrates]? We believe the answer to this question is NO, because: . . . (2)* **Roe vs. Wade** *(the law of the land) neither requires abortions nor prohibits them, but makes them permissible with certain restrictions. (3) The women who choose to have an abortion are free moral agents responsible before Almighty God for their actions, including the exercise of the rights of their innocent, unborn child.*

So say the deacons of one giant Southern Baptist church. I have already considered the argument that *Roe v. Wade* is not really morally evil because it does not actually compel abortions. Let us go to reason #3 in the critics' list. Change the word "abortion" to "murder," and allow the child to be out of the womb for five seconds. We get this bit of ethical wisdom: "The women who choose to murder their newborn children are free moral agents responsible before Almighty God for their actions, including the exercise of the rights of their innocent, newborn child." Are you in agreement?

No? Then why should you take seriously the moral perspective of the first version? Why should God take it seriously?

What is the difference between murdering an infant who is five seconds out of the womb and murdering an infant five hours earlier? Or five days? Or five weeks? I will tell you what the difference is: *safe pulpits.* For now.

Let us consider the argument based on the woman's "free moral agent" thesis. This is a real sleight-of-hand (tongue?) argument. The deacons have imported the idea of "pro-choice" abortionists into the church by changing the phrase to "free moral agent." This is one more example of how Christians baptize the language and ideas of secular humanism.

Is a murderer an equally "free moral agent"? This church's deacons implicitly say so. Is "free moral agency" under God a license from God to escape the God-ordained civil sanction of public execution for murder (Gen. 9:5)? The U.S. Supreme Court has eliminated this sanction, or any sanction, and this diaconate has now baptized the Court's decision. They are saying, in principle, that the U.S. Supreme Court is the highest court in America; God's Supreme Court gains jurisdiction only after we die.

Was Pharaoh's court the highest court in Egypt?

I would also ask this: Is it lawful for Christians in Communist China to resist their civil magistrates today, since abortion *is* compulsory there after the first child? Would these deacons say that it is immoral for Western Christians to smuggle Bibles into Red China, as well as tracts showing the Chinese ways to resist this evil compulsory abortion law?

Are Christians so downright blind today that they cannot see what will come next if *Roe v. Wade* isn't overturned? Will the civil magistrates have to drag our wives and daughters to the compulsory abortion mills before these shepherds figure out that *Roe v. Wade* is in fact only stage one in the humanists' program of legalized euthanasia? In Holland, mercy killings have now been legalized; first abortion was legalized, then the murder of the aged. But these shepherds still have not caught on.

In 1925, the humanists said that all they wanted to do was to get Darwinian evolution taught in the public schools alongside the creation story. "That's all we're asking. We promise. Trust us!" Christians did, too. Surprise!

Bait and Switch

Armed resistance by Christians is illegitimate except when a lesser magistrate authorizes it. By what authority do these anti-abortion interposers operate?

Two different issues are being raised. The first is armed interposition. The second is non-violent interposition. The two are not the same. It is biblically illegitimate to require members of the second group (non-violent resisters) to be bound by the biblical laws governing the first group (armed revolutionaries). To argue that they are so bound is deliberately to mix separate legal categories.

If the physical interposers who block the doorway of an abortion clinic remain peaceful, they are not required by God to seek authorization by any civil magistrate. Did the apostles seek the authorization of the "lesser magistrate" when they entered the Temple and synagogues and preached what the Jewish priests and Roman rulers had forbidden? Obviously not. They necessarily broke rebellious man's unrighteous laws when they obeyed God's law. They suffered the subsequent beatings, but they continued to disobey the unrighteous laws. They had been instructed by Jesus Christ to remain in Jerusalem (Acts 1:4). Jerusalem was to be given one more generation to repent, and the apostles were not dissuaded from this assignment. It overrode all questions of state-authorized preaching.

I am not talking about armed resistance with lethal weapons. The "armed resistance" I am talking about in this book is putting your arms over your head while an abortion-protecting policeman is beating you with a club.

What I am arguing here is that critics who mix the two categories of interposition have a hidden agenda. They did not come to this conclusion on the basis of evidence in the biblical texts.

Biblical Morality Is Not for Pagan Societies

Proverbs 24:11 applies only to rulers, and only in Christian nations, not to individual Christians in non-Christian nations.

Consider the context of Proverbs 24:11. The setting is that of a moral coward who refuses to help the defenseless. "If thou faint in the day of adversity, thy strength is small. If thou forbear to deliver them that are drawn unto death, and those that are ready to be slain; If thou sayest, Behold, we knew it not; doth not he that pondereth the heart consider it? and he that keepeth thy soul, doth not he know it? and shall not he render to every man according to his works?" (Proverbs 24:10-12).

I can well understand why any Christian who reads these verses and who knows what is going on behind the closed doors of an abortion clinic should feel a sense of shame. I know I do. But at least I am not offering this kind of intellectual defense of my own shameful inaction:

> The proverbs are for life in the covenant community. The Bible is not a book of moralisms that can be applied everywhere and anytime in total disregard for their . . . covenantal and redemptive context in Christ. These proverbs do not work outside of Christ. Their primary concern is the covenant (Christian) community.

Well, then, what about the Proverbs' "secondary" concern? Don't they count for something? Dead silence. (Dead religion. Faith without works is dead.)

The Queen of Sheba came to visit Solomon and was impressed. "And she gave the king an hundred and twenty talents of gold, and of spices very great store, and precious stones: there came no more such abundance of spices as these which the queen of Sheba gave to king Solomon" (I Kings 10:10). Why? Because of his wisdom.

What about the evangelism aspect of Deuteronomy 4:5-8?

> Behold, I have taught you statutes and judgments, even as the LORD my God commanded me, that ye should do so in the land whither ye go to possess it. Keep therefore and do them; for this is your wisdom and your understanding in the sight of the nations, which shall hear all these statutes, and say, Surely this great nation is a wise and understanding people. For what nation is there so great, who hath God so nigh unto them, as the LORD our God is

in all things that we call upon him for? And what nation is there so great, that hath statutes and judgments so righteous as all this law, which I set before you this day?

The fact that biblical law applies to a biblical covenantal social context is precisely why biblical law *is* applicable to pagan societies. They, too, are required by God to covenant with Him and restructure their institutions and laws accordingly.

What the critic who wrote these words about the inapplicability of the Book of Proverbs to pagan societies is trying to do is to deflect our eyes from the judicial authority of the whole Bible over all Christians, all mankind, in all settings, throughout all of history. *This critic is an antinomian who has concealed his arguments in the language of covenant theology.*

To say that the Book of Proverbs is only applicable in a so-called "covenantal context" of a covenantally redeemed civilization is another way of saying that the Book of Proverbs has been judicially irrelevant throughout most of history and in almost all areas on earth. When has such a covenantal context existed in history? Not very often. Does this mean that the entire Book of Proverbs has no legal standing in God's eyes until a society becomes formally covenanted to God? That it *should* have no legal standing in Christians' eyes before their society becomes formally covenanted to God? This is exactly what the critic is saying.

Let us recognize this argument for what it is: *the standard liberal theological line.* Baptized, of course. It is the Bible-thumping fundamentalist's version of the old liberal pitch: "The laws of the primitive Hebrews were applicable only in the context of an agricultural community, etc., etc." Christians have been hit with this moral relativism for over a hundred years. This is what such an interpretation of the Bible is: *moral relativism,* pure and simple. *This is humanistic antinomianism wrapped in covenantal swaddling clothes.* This is the language of a person who has, in the words of Proverbs 24:10, fainted in the day of adversity, and whose strength is small.

Enforcing Righteous Law Is Irrelevant

Before abortion will stop, hearts must be changed from rebellion against God to love for God through faith in Christ. . . . Our ultimate goal is not a constitutional amendment, which will change nothing.

Really? Then why did no nation legalize abortion until after World War II? Were they all Christian nations before World War II?

If we have to wait until almost all people in the U.S. are converted to saving faith in Jesus Christ before we can stop abortion in America, then only the postmillennialist can have any confidence that legalized abortion will ever be stopped, and only then during the millennium. Everyone else should give up the fight, this sheepfold theologian is telling us. There is no earthly hope. Abortion will not be stopped this side of the millennium.

This is just one more excuse for sitting safely inside the walls of your local church, or handing out tracts on the Bill of Rights-protected sidewalk. It is an excuse supported by one of the flimsiest arguments imaginable, namely, that passing a law changes nothing.

Let us substitute the words "selling cocaine to minors" for the word "abortion." Here is what we get: "Before the sale of cocaine to minors will stop, hearts must be changed from rebellion against God to love for God through faith in Christ. . . . Our ultimate goal is not a constitutional amendment, which will change nothing."

Or how about child pornography? "Before the sale of child pornography will stop, hearts must be changed from rebellion against God to love for God through faith in Christ. . . . Our ultimate goal is not a constitutional amendment, which will change nothing."

A constitutional amendment changes nothing? The civil law changes nothing? Well, the enforcement of Federal laws surely changed segregation in the South, and changed it within a single decade, 1960-70. What kind of theology teaches that civil law changes nothing? Sheepfold theology.

I will tell you what righteous civil law changes: *evil public acts*. This is all that civil law is supposed to change. It does not save men's souls; it is intended to change men's public behavior.

Those who tell us that laws change nothing are taking up the old liberal line: "You can't pass laws against pornography. They won't change anything." How about this one? "Don't bother to pass a law against prostitution; it won't change anything." Or how about this one: "It does no good to pass laws against selling cocaine to children in exchange for homosexual favors. That won't change anything."

Lawfully execute a dozen abortionist physicians, and it will change plenty. Make them legally liable to the point of personal bankruptcy if their operations permanently injure a woman, and you will see lots of change. Very rapid change.[1]

Men do not need to be converted to Christ in order for them to change their outward ways. Nineveh was not converted to the God of the Bible by Jonah's preaching. Nineveh, the capital city of Assyria, later invaded Israel and carried the Israelites away into pagan captivity. Nineveh remained the capital of a covenant-breaking empire. But almost overnight, in response to Jonah's message, Nineveh changed its outward behavior, and in so doing, avoided the promised external judgment of God that Jonah had predicted. (And when the judgment did not come, Jonah was depressed.)

This is what the anti-abortionist protesters are trying to do: *avoid the external, national judgment of God.* But the pre-whale Jonahs of our day are telling them to go to Tarshish instead. Tarshish is so much less controversial. Tarshish is so much safer.

---

1. While it is true that from a strictly biblical standpoint, the mother is herself a murderer, the primary goal is to stop the abortions, not seek judicial vengeance. As Christian values progressively dominate a society, legislators can steadily escalate the civil sanctions against abortion. For now, however, a more appropriate tactic than civil prosecution of these mothers — which will not be sustained in court — is to use injured mothers to put the abortionists out of business. If we do not begin to save the lives of the physicians' targeted victims, God may not give this nation sufficient time for Christians to change its legal structure by political mobilization.

Until you move out to sea, and the storm starts.

"Living the Gospel" in Temporary Safety

Only the preaching and teaching and living of the gospel of Christ in the power of the Holy Spirit is able to awaken an apostate church to repentance and faith.

This is exactly what the anti-abortion activists say. *Living the gospel of Christ means doing what you can do effectively that may save judicially innocent lives.* But for our "deeply concerned" antinomian critic, living for the gospel apparently means sitting safely in the sanctuary and praying prayers in private. And running for political office, of course.

Where are the imprecatory psalms in all this? Where are preachers who are willing to stand before their congregations on Sunday morning, praying down the visible curses of God on named abortionists, named civil magistrates, and all U. S. Supreme Court justices who voted for *Roe v. Wade?* Where is Psalm 83 in their churches' liturgies? When I at last locate some "safety first" critic of non-violent confrontation who is at least involved in weekly picketing and praying public imprecatory psalms as part of his church's weekly worship service, I will be more inclined to take his arguments seriously. Until then, I prefer to reject these arguments as self-justifying pious gush.

The Invisible Gospel

Preaching the gospel is sufficient to change all things. It does no good to look for physical solutions, such things as demonstrations or planned civil rebellion. Preaching is sufficient.

To which I answer, with James: "What doth it profit, my brethren, though a man say he hath faith, and have not works? Can faith save him? If a brother or sister be naked, and destitute of daily food, And one of you say unto them, Depart in peace, be ye warmed and filled; notwithstanding ye give them not those things which are needful to the body; what doth it profit? Even so faith, if it hath not works, is dead, being alone. Yea, a man may say, Thou hast faith, and I have works: shew me thy faith without thy works, and I will shew thee my faith by my works" (James 2:14-18).

So, "It does no good to look for physical solutions, such things as demonstrations or planned civil rebellion. Preaching is sufficient." This is what I call spiritualizing away the Scriptures. This is a form of fundamentalist mysticism (what philosophers used to call neo-Platonism). It is a withdrawal from the hard choices and dangerous commitments of life. But most of all, it is a denial of the Old Testament and the Epistle of James. It is a denial of God's real-world covenant, yet all in the name of faithful service to God.

Speak Softly and Carry No Stick

Then, when Moses entered Egypt again, forty years later, he was armed only with the powerful word of Jehovah. And that was all he needed to liberate his people from bondage.

I remember something about a rod that turned into a serpent and ate the serpents of Pharaoh's magicians. I also recall something about Moses touching the Nile River with this rod and turning the Nile to blood. There was something about dust into lice, too, and day into darkness, and several other unpleasant events.

Either the critic wants us to remain content by speaking words of visible impotence — no lice, no frogs, no fiery hail from heaven — or else he wants us to wait for God to turn us into "heap big medicine men." It does not matter which, just so long as we avoid trouble with the civil magistrate.

What the non-violent interposers want us to do is to pray, preach, hand out tracts, and block doorways. The critic forgets that we can pray with our eyes open. He forgets that we can pray while our heads are being clubbed, and while we are being hauled off to the local jail. We can also pray when we insist on a jury trial. We can pray while we are writing checks — yes, even non-tax-deductible checks — to the hard-pressed families of those men who have been put in jail or prison for their public testimony.

But not the critic. What he wants is prayer in the solitude of his prayer closet. There are no lawsuits in prayer closets. It is nice and safe there. For now.

Let the Other Congregations Repent First

The church must repent first, if America is to be saved from divine judgment, and if America is going to stop killing babies.

Of course "the church" must repent. (When a pastor says "the church," he really means the church across the street that just persuaded three families to leave his church and transfer their membership. A "dangerously radical church" is the church across town whose stand against abortion recently persuaded his church's only tithing millionaire to transfer.) Judgment surely begins at the house of the Lord. "For the time is come that judgment must begin at the house of God: and if it first begin at us, what shall the end be of them that obey not the gospel of God?" (I Peter 4:17).

Question: What is a tactic of non-violent, anti-abortion, bodily interposition, if not the first stage of the church's repentance? Must repentance forever be confined strictly to the heart? Must it be forever trapped inside of the local church's four walls? Is it limited to favorable write-ups in the society column of the local newspaper rather than critical editorials and front page headlines? Isn't repentance supposed to be a *public* turning away from sin?

And isn't tactically unnecessary cowardice in the face of legalized murder a sin to be repented of publicly?

God's national covenant works differently from the way this critic thinks. If America is going to gain enough time to repent, Christians had better persuade the Supreme Court to reverse *Roe v. Wade*, or Congress to remove the Court's jurisdiction over abortion (for which there is Constitutional precedent: *Ex parte McCardle*, 1868).

The Civil Magistrate Is Never To Be Resisted

It is my contention that when Jesus told His disciple to put up his sword (Matthew 26:47-56), that He was not simply forbidding the use of force or violence, but that He was telling him not to resist the civil magistrate at all!

So much for this entire book and every Bible passage cited. So much for the apostles' refusing to cease preaching. So much for the early church's resistance to the Roman Empire. So much for the Protestant Reformation. And most of all, so much for millions of murdered babies yet to come. And go.

The Sheriff Will Not Be Our Friend

Operation Rescue will make the sheriff the enemy of our pro-life efforts. He is not our enemy, unless he refuses to enforce the law of God.

Here is double-speak for Christians. Orwell named it well. "Truth is Falsehood." "Freedom is Tyranny." "The Sheriff is Our Friend When He Is Our Enemy."

Follow the logic of this endless-loop cassette: "The sheriffs of this land without exception are refusing to enforce the law of God regarding murder. They are therefore our enemies. But Operation Rescue is the real culprit. It is making the sheriffs our enemies. They are not our enemies, except when they refuse to enforce the law of God. The sheriffs of this land. . . ." Round and round it goes. It is designed to make Christians dizzy. Christians who are dizzy will sit tight, right where they are, culturally impotent.

Think back to Birmingham, Alabama. The year is 1963. Blacks are marching in the streets to get their Constitutionally guaranteed rights enforced by law. They want to be allowed to vote.

Do you remember the photograph that encapsulated that historic confrontation? I do. It was photo of the police dogs of Birmingham being turned loose on black protesters. That one photograph torpedoed the South's Bad Old Cause. *Click.*

But any use of the media to promote the pro-life cause is bad, we are told. It is unbiblical. "We must look for no short-cuts, no new strategies or tactics. We must not allow our resources and energies to be drained away by exciting and dramatic methods to stop abortion. . . ."

And again: "Beware of being pressured by the emphasis that civil rebellion generates 'media coverage' and increases social tension and upheaval so as to bring the abortion question into the public awareness." Furthermore, "that is Marxist and Hegelian tactics."

To which I answer: *Click.*

The name of the sheriff who ran the Birmingham operation will live in infamy, for his name was "media perfect": *Bull Connor.*

Now, let us restructure our critic's assertion. It is 1963 in Alabama. We are assured by the pastor of Laodicea Covenant Church that "Public protests will make Sheriff Connor the enemy of our civil rights efforts. He is not our enemy, unless he refuses to enforce the law of God."

I get tired of hearing such nonsense, offered in the name of covenant theology. So, let us turn to a decidedly non-covenant theologian, from the very same city as our supposed experts on the covenant: Atlanta.

Murder Is Wrong, Except When Convenient

We believe that abortion is wrong in cases other than where the physical life or mental well-being of the mother is at stake.

Wow! What a moral wall of resistance against evil!

As always, we need to alter this pastor's words only slightly. The child is now five seconds out of the womb. Change "abortion" to "infanticide." We discover this "breakthrough principle" of biblical ethics: "We believe that infanticide is wrong in cases other than where the physical life or mental well-being of the mother is at stake."

Now the child is five years old. "We believe that murdering young children is wrong in cases other than where the physical life or mental well-being of the mother is at stake."

Now the former child is 80 years old and infirm. You know what is coming: "We believe that euthanasia for the terminally ill is wrong in cases other than where the financial solvency of the Medicare program is at stake." But Pastor X cannot see that this is surely coming. Maybe because he is not yet 70.

This man prides himself on having been a white pastor in the civil rights marches of the early 1960's. He did the right thing back then. His adopted cause was just. But was the legal right of blacks to vote in 1963 of greater moral and eternal importance than the legal right of babies to be born today?

I can almost hear Bull Connor now: "We believe that racial discrimination is wrong in cases other than where Southern white supremacy is at stake."

A quarter century ago, Pastor X marched illegally in the streets in Alabama, braving billy clubs, all for the sake of black voter registration. But now what? Now that he has a huge church, white hair, and a national television ministry, what is his moral stand? "I answer that we are providing action rather than marching in reaction. . . . We provide programs for unwed mothers. . . . And we do it on our grounds, not illegally in the streets. For this we do not apologize."

I am not asking him to apologize. I am simply asking him to stop writing his self-justifying letters to the *Atlanta Constitution* — letters critical of Operation Rescue.

May God protect each of us from the morally fatal lure of hoped-for respectability in the eyes of murderers and their moral accomplices in the pews. May God also protect us from the false dilemma of "either/or," where we are asked to choose between providing homes for unwed mothers and refusing to challenge legalized murder in the doorways and streets of our local towns and cities.

Where Will It All End?

Where does civil disobedience stop?

Where does moral cowardice stop? Where does full-time Christian blindness to humanism's long-term program of legalized murder stop? In the Gulag Archipelago? In the gas chambers? Or in Atlanta? I prefer to see Christian moral cowardice and judicial blindness stopped in Atlanta. I can see where we are headed if they persist.

We Must Honor God's Word

We must let God's word speak the truth to us about this matter of civil disobedience.

Amen! You have this book in front of you. You may even have read it. What do you honestly think God's word teaches? And having made up your mind, "be ye doers of the word, and not hearers only, deceiving your own selves" (James 1:22).

A Letter to a "Concerned" Critic

Perhaps some of these critics are sincere people. They want to lead other Christians in the paths of righteousness. They have gone into print against non-violent protesters, so they obviously think they have the right to lead others in this matter.

On the other hand, maybe they are merely opposed to illegal public confrontation and not just providing self-justification for their own lack of commitment.

Here is a good test. If you are being asked to believe a line of argumentation anything like the arguments that I have covered in this appendix, you need to get some idea of the pastor's own commitment to the anti-abortion cause apart from the question of civil disobedience. You need to write him a letter. It should go something like this:

Pastor Reuben Lamb
Safety First Christian Church
Meroz, Georgia

Dear Pastor Lamb:

I have read with interest your criticisms of the Operation Rescue movement. Because you "went public" on this issue, I believe I have the right to ask you about several related details. I would like to get a few questions answered before I make up my mind about the nature and motivation of your criticisms.

First, on average over the past year, how many hours per week did you personally spend in anti-abortion picket lines or in counselling pregnant unwed mothers?

Second, what percentage of your local church's income was designated to the support of various anti-abortion protests or programs?

Third, How many times during the last twelve months have you publicly prayed an imprecatory psalm or its equivalent during your church's morning worship service? What are the names of the local abortionists and civil magistrates whom you named publicly in these prayers?

Fourth, have any members of your local congregation had abortions during your pastorate? If any, then of those who did not publicly repent in front of the congregation, how many were excommunicated?

Fifth, does your church have a policy of officially encouraging the adoption of children born to unmarried mothers? Could you send me details of your program?

I realize that not many pastors and churches do many of these things, but not many pastors "go public" with criticisms of Operation Rescue, either.

Very truly yours,

If you do not get a frank, non-hostile response, you know that you are dealing with a wolf in sheep's clothing. Or a sheep in battle fatigues.

I am reminded of General Patton's speech at the beginning of the movie, "Patton." He announced to his troops that someday, "your grandchildren will ask you what you did in the great World War II, and you won't have to have to say, 'I shoveled [   ] in Louisiana.'"

We have a lot of "concerned" pastors these days who are content to cling to their shovels. They call this biblical trench warfare. And when they start shoveling, it really flies.

Conclusion

As a person committed to covenant theology, I am appalled at the intellectually lightweight and Scripturally bankrupt sheepfold manifestos that I have seen so far. The ones offered in the name of God's covenant are the greatest embarrassment to me. Their arguments do not differ significantly from the manifestos that have poured out of "Fundamentalists for Pro-Life, Sort Of" pastors.

The intellectual bankruptcy of some of the published criticisms of Operation Rescue does not automatically legitimize Operation Rescue. We should not be lured into the mistake of getting on a controversial bandwagon just because those who say we should stay home are not intellectually or theologically capable of defending their negative position.

I have discussed Operation Rescue as a real-world example of non-violent Christian resistance. I see nothing wrong with what they have done, as of late 1988. I have serious reservations about where the group may be in a few years, or where its radical spin-offs may be. But in a time of social, moral, political, and medical turmoil, as the 1990's will almost certainly be, it is impossible to be sure where any group will be.

What we need from Operation Rescue is an official statement of tactical and strategic faith. We need a statement that under no circumstances will Operation Rescue or any of its official representatives call for armed resistance to civil authority without public support from a lesser magistrate. We need a statement that violence will not be initiated by Operation Rescue groups against the bodies of private citizens, except for unarmed physical interposition: separating murderous physicians from their clients and targeted unborn victims. We need also a statement that the deliberate destruction of the actual tools used by licensed murderers in their crimes will endanger only the property and not any person.

As a matter of tactics, it would be nice to hear that Operation Rescue has advised all participants of the need to fight this battle through the courts, and has recommended to everyone who gets arrested that he or she should immediately give name, address, and other pertinent information to the authorities, because he or she intends to demand a jury trial. What this nation needs is about 20,000 jury trials a year litigating this life-and-death issue. Eventually, the U.S. Supreme Court will reverse *Roe v. Wade* on some technicality. If we give the Court 20,000 or so cases a year to choose from, the Court will discover a way out of its dilemma, preferably short of civil war. For more information about Operation Rescue, contact them at

Operation Rescue
P.O. Box 1180
Binghampton, NY 13902

It is not necessarily immoral or inherently cowardly to refuse to get involved in protests like these. People are told by God to count the costs. There may be more cost-effective ways of dealing with abortion. For example, Charles Stanley's First Baptist Church in Atlanta is supporting a legal effort by the Atlanta organization, Family Concerns, Inc., to bring malpractice suits against abortion clinics. The churches and physicians working with Family Concerns, Inc. are actively seeking the names of abortion clinic victims. This strategy is excellent. If successful, it will raise malpractice insurance premiums to such a level that the state-licensed murderers will have to go into full-time healing in order to make a decent living. I have donated money to help support this worthy effort.

Abortion Lawsuit Project
Family Concerns, Inc.
P.O. Box 550168
Atlanta, GA 30355

Nevertheless, if it is not abortion, it will be the licensing of Christian schools, or home schools, or some other intolerable evil. Christianity is under attack. There is a war on. It is time for the Reubenites to turn off their word processors, go fishing with Dan, and leave those of us in God's army to fight the Amalekites without having to pull Israelite arrows out of our backs.

Appendix B

RESOURCES

There are a large number of excellent pro-life and charitable organizations that you can look to for help in your struggle for life and truth. Each has a unique area of specialty. Each has literature, presentations, services, resources, and opportunities that you can take advantage of, and each is deserving of your prayerful and financial support.

The following list is by no means comprehensive, but it should give you a good start.

Americans Against Abortion
P.O. Box 40
Lindale, TX 75771

American Life League (ALL)
P.O. Box 490
Stafford, VA 22554

American Rights Coalition
P.O. Box 487
Chattanooga, TN 37401

Americans United for Life
343 South Dearborn, Suite 1804
Chicago, IL 60604

Birthright
11235 South Western Avenue
Chicago, IL 60643

Black Americans for Life
419 7th Street, NW, Suite 402
Washington, DC 20004

Christian Action Council (CAC)
422 C Street, NE
Washington, DC 20002

Couple to Couple League
P.O. Box 11084
Cincinnati, OH 45211

161

Committee to Protect the
Family Foundation
8001 Forbes Place, Suite 102
Springfield, VA 22151

Concerned Women for America
(CWA)
122 C Street, NW, Suite 800
Washington, DC 20001

Eagle Forum
P. O. Box 618
Alton, IL 62002

Family Research Council
515 Second Street, NE
Washington, DC 20002

Focus on the Family
801 Corporae Center Drive
Pomona, CA 91764

Free Congress Research and
Education Foundation
721 Second Street, NE
Washington, DC 20002

Heart Light
P. O. Box 8513
Green Bay, WI 54308

HELP Services Women's Center
P. O. Box 1141
Humble, TX 77338

Human Life Foundation
150 East 35th Street
New York, NY 10157

Human Life International
7845-E Airpark Road
Gaithersburg, MD 20879

Liberty Federation
505 Second Street, NE
Washington, DC 20002

Liberty Godparent Foundation
P. O. Box 27000
Lynchburg, VA 24506

Lifenet
P. O. Box 185066
Fort Worth, TX 76181-0066

Life Advocates
4848 Guiton, Suite 209
Houston, TX 77027

March for Life Education
and Defense Fund
P. O. Box 90330
Washington, DC 20090

March Houston for Life
P. O. Box 207
Spring, TX 77383

Moral Majority
2020 Tate Springs Road
Lynchburg, VA 24501

National Right to Life Committee
419 7th Street, NW, Suite 402
Washington, DC 20004

Operation Blessing
CBN Center
Virginia Beach, VA 23463

Orthodox Christians for Life
P. O. Box 805
Melville, NY 11747

Pro-Life Action League
6160 North Cicero Avenue
Chicago, IL 60646

Pro-Life Action Ministries
611 South Snelling Avenue
St. Paul, MN 55116

Rutherford Institute
P. O. Box 510
Manassas, VA 22110

Sex Respect
P. O. Box 349
Bradley, IL 60915

Why Wait?
P. O. Box 1000
Dallas, TX 75221

Women Exploited (WE)
2100 West Ainsley
Chicago, IL 60640

Women Exploited By Abortion
(WEBA)
202 South Andrews
Three Rivers, MI 49093

A number of organizations specialize in distributing pro-life books, tracts, films, and slide presentations. Again, the following list is by no means comprehensive, but it should point you in the right direction.

American Portrait Films
1695 West Crescent Avenue,
Suite 500
Anaheim, CA 92801

Catholics United for Life
(CUL)
New Hope, KY 40052

Christian WorldView (CWV)
P. O. Box 185066
Fort Worth, TX 76181-0066

Couple to Couple League
3621 Clenmore Avenue
Cincinnati, OH 45211

Crossway Books
9825 West Roosevelt Road
Westchester, IL 60153

Dominion Press
P. O.Box 8204
Fort Worth, TX 76124

Hayes Publishing
6304 Hamilton Avenue
Cincinnati, OH 45224

The Human Life Review
150 East 35th Street
New York, NY 10157

Life Cycle Books
2205 Danforth Avenue
Toronto, Ontario M4L1K4

LifeNet
P. O. Box 185066
Fort Worth, TX 76181-0066

Michael Fund
400 Penn Center Blvd.,

Room 1022
Pittsburgh, PA 15235

Operation Rescue
P. O. Box 1180
Binghamton, NY 13902

Servant Publications
P. O. Box 8617
Ann Arbor, MI 48107

Thoburn Press
P. O. Box 6941
Tyler, TX 75711

Wolgemuth & Hyatt, Publishers
P. O. Box 1941
Brentwood, TN 37027

There is nothing as valuable as primary source documents. You can write to the various pro-abortion, anti-family organizations below and receive some of the most remarkable literature you could ever imagine.

Abortion Rights Association
100 East Ohio
Chicago, IL 60611

Alan Guttmacher Institute
360 Park Avenue, South
New York, NY 10010

National Abortion Rights
Action League
825 15th Street, NW
Washington, DC 20005

National Organization
for Women
425 13th Street, NW
Washington, DC 20004

Planned Parenthood Federation
of America
515 Madison Avenue
New York, NY 10022

Planned Parenthood-
World Population
810 7th Avenue
New York, NY 10019

Religious Coalition for
Abortion Rights
100 Maryland Avenue, NE
Washington, DC 20002

BIBLIOGRAPHY

When a Christian takes the first step in non-violent protesting, he needs to ask himself these questions:

"What am I being asked to do?"
"Why am I being asked to do this?"
"Am I biblically justified in doing this?"
"What is the likely cost of my doing this?"
"What is the likely outcome of what we are doing?"

There have been many protest groups in history that have claimed to be Christian, some good and some evil. The apocalyptic communist revolutionaries of the thirteenth and fourteenth centuries were evil. The communist and polygamous radical Anabaptist revolutionaries of Luther's day were evil. So, the Christian must ask himself this question: *By what standard?* By what standard is the particular protest group evaluating its legal and moral right, as well as the tactical and strategic wisdom, of organizing this protest? By what standard is it imposing its discipline? By what standard does it pick its targets?

To answer these questions, you need a theology. You need *covenant theology*. No other theology offers equally consistent, Bible-based answers. This theology provides a comprehensive world-and-life view, one which incorporates a theory of obedience (covenant-keeping) and a theory of disobedience (covenantbreaking). It is the Bible which must provide us with our standards and our definitions, not humanism, whether secular or Christian (natural law theory).

165

166 *When Justice Is Aborted*

The following books will serve as an introduction to covenant theology. They provide the Christian community with an explicitly biblical approach to social and political problems.

Biblical Covenant

Sutton, Ray. *That You May Prosper: Dominion By Covenant.* Tyler, Texas: Institute for Christian Economics, 1987.

_____ . *Covenant Renewal.* Monthly newsletter. Published by the Institute for Christian Economics, P. O. Box 8000, Tyler, Texas 75711.

Biblical World-and-Life View

DeMar, Gary and Leithart, Peter. *The Reduction of Christianity.* Ft. Worth, Texas: Dominion Press, 1988.

North, Gary. *Dominion and Common Grace: The Biblical Basis of Progress.* Tyler, Texas: Institute for Christian Economics, 1987

_____ . *Is the World Running Down? Crisis in the Christian Worldview.* Tyler, Texas: Institute for Christian Economics, 1988.

_____ . *Liberating Planet Earth: An Introduction to Biblical Blueprints.* Ft. Worth, Texas: Dominion Press, 1987.

_____ . *Moses and Pharaoh: Dominion Religion vs. Power Religion.* Tyler, Texas: Institute for Christian Economics, 1985.

_____ . *Unconditional Surrender: God's Program for Victory.* Tyler, Texas: Institute for Christian Economics, (1981) 1988.

_____ . *75 Bible Questions Your Instructors Pray You Won't Ask.* Tyler, Texas: Institute for Christian Economics, (1984) 1988.

Olasky, Marvin N. *The Press and Abortion, 1938-1988.* Lawrence Erlbaum Associates, Hillsdale, NJ, 1988

Biblical Civil Government

DeMar, Gary. *God and Government.* 3 volumes. Atlanta, Georgia: American Vision, 1982-86.

——————. *Ruler of the Nations: Biblical Blueprints for Government.* Ft. Worth, Texas: Dominion Press, 1987.

Grant, George. *The Changing of the Guard: Biblical Blueprints for Political Action.* Ft. Worth, Texas: Dominion Press, 1987.

North, Gary. *Healer of the Nations: Biblical Blueprints for International Relations.* Ft. Worth, Texas: Dominion Press, 1987.

——————. *Political Polytheism: The Myth of Pluralism.* Tyler, Texas: Institute for Christian Economics, 1989.

Secular Humanism

Humanist Manifestos I and II. Buffalo, New York: Prometheus Books, 1973.

Hitchcock, James. *What Is Secular Humanism?* Ann Arbor, Michigan: Servant Books, 1982.

North, Gary. *Conspiracy: A Biblical View.* Ft. Worth, Texas: Dominion Press, 1986. (Co-published by Crossway Books.)

——————. "From Cosmic Purposelessness to Humanistic Sovereignty," Appendix A, in Gary North, *The Dominion Covenant: Genesis.* 2nd ed.; Tyler, Texas: Institute for Christian Economics, 1987.

Rushdoony, Rousas John. *The Messianic Character of American Education.* Phillipsburg, New Jersey: Presbyterian & Reformed, 1963.

Whitehead, John. *The Second American Revolution.* Elgin, Illinois: David C. Cook Pub. Co., 1982.

——————. *The Stealing of America.* Westchester, Illinois: Crossway, 1982.

Biblical Law

Bahnsen, Greg L. *By This Standard: The Authority of God's Law Today.* Tyler, Texas: Institute for Christian Economics, 1985.

—————— . *Theonomy in Christian Ethics.* 2nd ed.; Phillipsburg, New Jersey: Presbyterian & Reformed, 1984.

Rushdoony, Rousas John. *The Institutes of Biblical Law.* Phillipsburg, New Jersey: Presbyterian & Reformed, 1973.

Rutherford, Samuel. *Lex, Rex; Or, The Law and the Prince.* Harrisonburg, Virginia: Sprinkle Publications, 1982. Reprint of 1827 edition. Originally published in 1644.

Christian Resistance

Calvin, John. *Institutes of the Christian Religion.* Book IV, Chapter 20. 1559 edition. Philadelphia: Westminster Press, 1960.

North, Gary. *Backward, Christian Soldiers?* Tyler, Texas: Institute for Christian Economics, 1984

—————— , editor. *Tactics of Christian Resistance. Christianity and Civilization, 3.* Tyler, Texas: Geneva Ministries, 1983.

—————— , editor. *The Theology of Christian Resistance. Christianity and Civilization, 2.* Tyler, Texas: Geneva Ministries, 1983.

Schaeffer, Francis. *A Christian Manifesto.* Westchester, Illinois: Crossway, 1981.

Stauffer, Ethelbert. *Christ and the Caesars.* Philadelphia: Westminster Press, 1955.

Christian Revolution

"Junius Brutus." *A Defence of Liberty Against Tyrants*, a translation of *Vindiciae Contra Tyrannos.* Gloucester, Massachusetts: Peter Smith, 1963. Originally published in 1579.

Douglas, J. D. *Light in the North: The Story of the Scottish Covenanters.* Grand Rapids, Michigan: William B. Eerdmans, 1964.

Fraser, Antonia. *Cromwell: The Lord Protector.* New York: Knopf, 1974.

Hall, Verna, editor. *The Christian History of the American Revolution: Consider and Ponder.* San Francisco, California: Foundation for American Christian Education, 1976.

Hill, Christopher. *Puritanism and Revolution: Studies in Interpretation of the English Revolution of the 17th Century.* New York: Schocken Books, (1958) 1964.

North, Gary, editor. Symposium on Christianity and the American Revolution. *The Journal of Christian Reconstruction,* Vol. III, Summer, 1976. Published by the Chalcedon Foundation, P. O. Box 158, Vallecito, California 95251.

Paul, Robert S. *The Lord Protector: Religion and Politics in the Life of Oliver Cromwell.* Grand Rapids, Michigan: William B. Eerdmans, 1955.

Ridley, Jasper. *John Knox.* New York: Oxford University Press, 1968.

Stevenson, David. *The Scottish Revolution, 1637-44: The Triumph of the Covenanters.* New York: St. Martins, 1973.

SCRIPTURE INDEX

OLD TESTAMENT

NEW TESTAMENT

INDEX

175

immorality, 67-68
imprecatory psalms, xiv, 91-92
infanticide, 155
inheritance, 107, 109, 117
injustice, 42, 45, 71
intercessors, 99
interposition
  doctrine of, 45, 94
  intercession, 99
  Jesus, 98
  physical, 97-99
  sanctions, 97, 99-100
  Israel, 9, 12
Issachar, 65

jail, xi, xiii
Jehoiakim, 87-88
Jeremiah, 84-88
Jericho, 53
Jeroboam, 14
Jerusalem, 36-37, 146
Jesus
  absent?, 29
  conviction of, 40
  departure of, 26-27
  disinherited, 110
  genealogy, 53
  interposer, 45
  interposition, 90, 98
  Lord of history, 29
  loyalty to, 22
  reconciliation, 123-24
  resurrection, 23, 27, 28
  salvation by, 22-23
  Second Coming, 23, 37
  throne, 28, 46
Jews, 2
Joash, 55
Johesheba, 55
John the Baptizer, 11
Jonah, 150
Joram, 55

Joshua, ix-x
jubilee year, 25
Judah, 84-90, 101
judge, 31-32
judgment day, 5
"Junius Brutus", 93
justice, 32, 65, 72, 76, 85
justification, 33, 111

kamikazes, 29-30, 140
King, Martin Luther, 66, 101
kingdom
  authority, 56
  continuity of, 35
  extension, 123
  extension of, 29
  principles, 26
Kline, Meredith G., 6-7

lamb, 110
Lamb (Rev.), 157-58
law
  boundaries, 51
  change, 5
  evangelism, 147-48
  God's, 4
  history &, 62
  irrelevant, 149-150
  natural, 128-29
  negative, 143-44
  rigor, 62
  source, 20
  work of, 47, 79
lawsuit, 11-12
leaven, 58
legal positivism, 63-65
letter, 157-58
Leviticus, 8
Lewis, C.S., 80, 130
Lex, Rex, 130
liberals, 137
lies, 52-56

Bible, 12-14
Darwinian, 64
Jeremiah, 89
standards, 4
changing laws, 5
psalms, xiv, 91-92
punishment (corporal), 51

Queen of Sheba, 147

Rahab, 53, 56, 115-16
Rapture, 30-31, 35, 135-36
reaction, 67, 68-73
Reagan, Ronald, xiii
reconciliation, 112, 123-24
reconstruction, 32
relativism, 148
religion
political, 21
Renaissance, 80
representation
evil, 58
voice of God, 41-43
(see also magistrates)
rescue mission, 36, 136
resistance, 145-46
sanctions, 53
resisting evil, 99
responsibility, 72
resurrection, 23, 27, 28
Jews, 57
retreat, 140
Reuben, 133-34, 137, 160
revival
comprehensive, 32-34, 38
lost souls, 33-34
technology, 32
revolution, 65, 87
Bible on, 103
right of, 52
righteous, 116
revolutionaries

inward, 21
rhetoric, 140
righteousness, 26, 66
rights, 5
riots, 66
risks, 53
Roe v. Wade, 37, 91, 107, 139, 143, 144-45, 160
Rome, 1, 15, 21
Rowe, Ed, xiv
rulers
hate God, 19-20
rebellion of, 19-20
Rushdoony, R.J., 15
Rutherford, Samuel, 130-31

Satan
breaking with, 115-16
bureaucracy, 48-49
continuity, 112-13
creative, 49
defensive, 28
discontinuity, 108-10
inheritance of, 113
judged, 27
kamikaze, 30
kingdom of, 117
tyrant, 55
sacraments, 48, 50, 105
Sadducees, 57
saint, 92, 105, 107, 122
salt, 120-21
salvation
social, 25-26, 66
state?, 52
salve, 23
sanctification, 33, 122-23, 124
sanctions, 90-94
interposition, 97
negative, 56
positive, 56
watchman, 92-93